An Old Man Remembering Birds

An Old Man Remembering Birds

Michael Baughman

Oregon State University Press   Corvallis

Library of Congress Cataloging-in-Publication Data

Names: Baughman, Mike, 1937- author.
Title: An old man remembering birds / Michael Baughman.
Description: Corvallis : Oregon State University Press, 2021.
Identifiers: LCCN 2021035205 | ISBN 9780870711541 (trade paperback) | ISBN
   9780870711558 (ebook)
Subjects: LCSH: Baughman, Mike, 1937– | Bird watcher—United
   States—Biography. | Bird watching—United States. | Human-animal
   relationships.
Classification: LCC QL677.5 .B39 2021 | DDC 598.072/34092 [B]—dc23
LC record available at https://lccn.loc.gov/2021035205

♾ This paper meets the requirements of ANSI/NISO Z39.48-1992
(Permanence of Paper).

First published in 2021 by Oregon State University Press
Printed in the United States of America

Oregon State University
OSU Press

Oregon State University Press
121 The Valley Library
Corvallis OR 97331-4501
541-737-3166 • fax 541-737-3170
www.osupress.oregonstate.edu

For Hilde—my love, my wife, my friend

An old terror . . . shook him—not the terror of the end of the world, but of the end, simply, of all he knew and loved, which would then exist only in his knowing, the little creature of his memory.

—Wendell Berry, *Remembering: A Novel*

One of the first conditions of happiness is that the link between Man and Nature shall not be broken.

—Leo Tolstoy

And when the birds arrived from the South, it was said they told pitiful stories about us poor wingless fools who had no choice but to stay behind and freeze.

—Linda Hogan, *Solar Storms*

I don't feed the birds because they need me; I feed the birds because I need them.

—Kathi Hutton, Birding Ohio Facebook Group posting

Contents

Prologue

Ornithologists formally study the physiology, ecology, behavior, and classification of birds. I'm not an ornithologist. What I've done for the better part of a century is simply watch and listen to birds, and move and live among them. In that process I've accumulated indelible memories, many of them narrated here. While birds are featured in these pages, other wild creatures also make appearances: coyotes, bobcats, orcas, rattlesnakes, skunks, bats, deer, elk, a mother bear with cubs.

My lifelong relationship with the natural world—for me, the real world—began with my great-grandfather, John Brant, whom I knew as Granddad Brant and was descended from Mohawk Chief Thayendanegea, aka Joseph Brant, who lived from 1743 to 1807. In 1912, Granddad Brant's unmarried nineteen-year-old daughter, Willa, died two or three days after giving birth to my mother. Granddad Brant and his wife Emma raised my mother on their western Pennsylvania farm.

My father and mother and I lived near Pittsburgh, where there were crowded neighborhoods, noisy streets, and grimy bridges over railroad tracks; and where, an hour or two after a snowfall on a winter day, the white landscape had been blackened with soot. When my mother and I visited the farm, as we often did, Granddad Brant taught me how to catch trout in the creek that ran through his land, and where to find birds and animals in the woods. He told me more than once that he hunted and fished because he saw it as the single feature of Mohawk life that he could keep alive. He never took me hunting with him, but when we searched for pheasants, I was frightened and excited every time by the sudden, powerful drumming of wings and the crowing of a brightly colored, long-tailed rooster pheasant flushing from cover.

Three years after World War Two ended and shortly after Granddad Brant died, my parents headed west, as many Americans did in those days. After brief stops in Dallas and Los Angeles, we ended up in Honolulu, where my father, in conjunction with labor unions, sold health insurance to plantation workers on all the major islands. For the next eight years I spent most of my free time in or near the Pacific Ocean, by far the most expansive wilderness on earth. The Waikiki beach boys, who taught tourists to surf small waves and took them on outrigger canoe rides, were the happiest humans I've ever known. They taught me to surf, bodysurf, spearfish, and paddle and steer koa wood outrigger racing canoes. I had sense enough to know I was growing up one of the luckiest boys alive. My happiest Hawaii days were surfing the summer breaks at Waikiki with frigate birds high overhead, slow black silhouettes circling in a clean blue sky.

While I was growing up in America, the woman I would marry, Hilde Eichhorn, was living in Bavaria, Germany's southernmost state, under very different circumstances. During the years I visited Granddad Brant on his Pennsylvania farm, she spent long nights sitting with her mother in a bomb shelter, her father a prisoner of war in Russia. As I surfed in Hawaii under circling frigate birds, she enjoyed roaming the postwar Bavarian countryside; but then, as now, it contained no truly wild country. On hikes through the woods or strolling between villages alongside fields of wheat and rye, people were virtually everywhere, but wildlife sightings were rare. Hunting and fishing privileges were limited, hard to come by and expensive, and restricted to the wealthy. No one in Hilde's family, though they were fine people, knew one species of bird from another; and they disliked birds in general due to the droppings left on windowsills, porch railings, and cars.

In 1960, as an enlisted soldier in the US Army stationed in Bamberg in northern Bavaria, I met Hilde at an International Students Club that had been founded after the war in a family home donated by Nina von Stauffenberg, widow of Colonel Klaus von Stauffenberg, who had been executed after his unsuccessful attempt to assassinate Hitler. We were married about a year later, and soon after that I was discharged from the army and we returned to the United States. After two years of working at menial jobs to pay my way through graduate school at San Francisco State, I took a job teaching writing and literature at Southern Oregon College in Ashland, Oregon.

This assignment took me to exactly where I wanted to be; but for Hilde, the wild and sparsely populated southern Oregon countryside was initially daunting. As we were driving through northern California backroads en route to Ashland in the late summer of 1966—there was no interstate freeway then—she broke out crying somewhere south of Yreka. Never in her life had she ever seen so much open country with no trace of civilization anywhere. I did my best to console her, to convince her that she'd adjust. And I was right. She became an expert fly-angler, cross-country skier, backpacker, and trail-runner; and she now loves wild country, and the birds and animals that live there, at least as much as I do.

Yes, I'm an old man, and I love birds because they're wild and free, and because of what they make me remember and think about. As I age, birds and the memories they evoke become increasingly important and ever more vivid; and, best of all, they impart comprehension. Though memories reveal no profound secrets, they allow me to better understand myself—what I've done, and why.

Regarding the material in this book: memories come to us randomly, seldom if ever in any plausible order. The most meaningful among them remain with us until we die. I present my recollections here much as they entered my mind and were processed there—not sequentially, but for me, in the end, strong, enriching, timeless.

A Hawk in the Sky

> I'd sooner, except for the penalties, kill a man than a hawk.
> —Robinson Jeffers, "Hurt Hawks"

In 2020, as I complete this memoir, Hilde and I are an old couple living through a hot, dry summer, doing the best we can. In town yesterday, many pedestrians were wearing masks—"particulate respirators"—to protect against the acrid smoke from the wildfires that surround us. Southern Oregon's Rogue Valley has been our home for more than half a century. We've raised our children here and helped them raise theirs, and uncontrollable wildfires are something new. Climate scientists advise us to get used to it. Two years ago and about two hundred miles to the south, the Camp Fire killed eighty-five Californians and destroyed nearly fourteen thousand homes.

A 2019 issue of *Harper's* magazine noted in its Findings section that "[p]ermafrost in the Canadian Arctic is thawing seventy years ahead of schedule, nitrous-oxide emissions from Arctic permafrost are twelve times higher than expected, and . . . existing models may underestimate underwater glacial melt by two orders of magnitude. Wildfires ravaged the Arctic, a meltwater lake appeared at the North Pole, and a European heat wave caused the loss of 12.5 billion tons of Greenlandic ice in a single day."

We have an acre of land a few miles outside Ashland. The fact that we look upon half of this acre as a private wildlife refuge should probably be regarded as a family joke, but we take the designation seriously. Within our refuge, birds nest in pines, firs, cedars, oaks, and fruit trees. Brush and high grass serve as ground cover for California ground squirrels and California valley quail. Deer visit, especially in October for fallen apples. In springtime, pairs of Canada geese, trailed by their goslings, march sedately under the trees and down a long hill toward a neighbor's farm pond. A roving flock of wild turkeys—Rio Grandes, transplants from Texas—feeds on grass and fallen acorns. Coyotes, bobcats, foxes, and skunks make occasional early morning appearances. Red-tailed hawks like to perch on the upper limbs of our tallest Douglas-fir, giving them a wide-ranging view of the valley floor.

Weather permitting, we spend an hour or more on the outdoor deck after breakfast, talking, sipping coffee, and watching wildlife, principally the birds. Our glass-topped table and comfortable chairs are no more than ten feet from the wide deck railing that serves as a platform feeder, and below the railing is a weathered stone statuette of St. Francis holding a bowl in his hands. Halfway between our table and St. Francis, a hummingbird feeder hangs from the deck's slatted roof. Every morning before breakfast, I stock both the railing and the proffered bowl with sunflower seeds, dried corn, flax, and millet. (The hummingbird feeder, visited daily from March through October, holds enough nectar so that it only needs a refill every couple of weeks.) Then, a few seconds after I ring a bell, squawking scrub jays swoop in to the limbs of a nearby oak tree, where they spend a few seconds checking things out before gliding down to feed.

Six years ago, an especially confident jay became a friend. On several consecutive mornings, when I brought out the seeds for the feeders, the assertive early bird was waiting for me, all alone on the railing. Eventually I decided to see how close I could get to the jay, and that morning I stayed right where I was after scattering the seeds and ringing the bell. From little more than a yard away, the bird stood looking at me, and I looked back. After a standoff of about a minute, the jay flew across the yard to perch on an oak tree limb, and I went back inside for my own breakfast.

After repeating this routine every day for a week, the bird lost all fear and began pecking at the seeds while I stood watching, close enough to touch it. Hilde and I ate pancakes for breakfast that day, and early the next morning I walked across the deck with the usual allotment of seeds in one hand and pieces of day-old pancake in the other. The jay stood on the railing looking at me, nodding its head up and down. I extended the pancake hand. The uneasy bird hopped back, looked me in the eye, then at the pancake pieces, and finally hopped forward and began to peck them up off my palm. I'd been worried that the jay might draw blood with its formidable bill, but it took the pieces daintily. From that day on, my friend took either pancake pieces or seeds from my hand whenever I made the offer.

As Kathy Hutton put it in her 2013 Facebook posting, Hilde and I feed the birds because we need them. To maintain the link between ourselves and Tolstoy's Nature—*our* Nature—we need to see them, hear them, simply know they're here. And we're by no means alone. At least 40 percent of Americans put out feed for wild birds, making this the most popular wildlife-related pastime in the country.

Despite the pastime's popularity, however, there's persistent speculation that feeding birds may ultimately be harmful to them. One often-cited concern is that overdependence on human handouts may endanger birds' subsequent ability to survive on their own, for example when a feeder goes unstocked for days or weeks at a time, in periods of extreme cold. Another concern is that concentrations of birds at feeders might facilitate the spread of communicable diseases.

Given these concerns, we found reassurance early on in a 1979 study directed by wildlife biologist Aelred Geis, then-head of the US Fish and Wildlife Service's Urban Wildlife Research Program. Geis's conclusions: "I don't agree with the prophets of doom regarding bird feeders. . . . My own observations prove to me that birds are more resourceful than a lot of people seem to think. Of course they'll take handouts gladly, but I think they can readjust to normal conditions when they have to. And birds in the wild—ducks and doves for instance—are often found in enormous concentrations, and no one talks about disease as far as they're concerned. . . . Anyone who feeds birds is bound to get a lot of pleasure out of it, and it has to enhance the public's concern for wildlife."

We were also reassured by our own bird-feeding circumstances and practices. Southern Oregon is on a latitude close to that of Rome, so we don't experience harsh winters here. We regularly clean both the deck railing and St. Francis bowl to reduce the remote possibility of spreading disease. Our feeders aren't within reach of any ground cover that could serve as a hiding place for opportunistic predators; and the seeds we set out each morning are usually gone by ten, noon at the latest. For most of the day, our birds are on their own.

Critics of stocking feeders sometimes compare it to the practice of attracting raptors with bait, dead or alive, usually in order to photograph them. But while two hawks fighting over a mouse might sustain injuries, the neighborhood birds that choose to visit our property come and go as they please, none of them suffering ill effects. Of the ten thousand species of birds that inhabit planet Earth, we can count on the following—along with hummingbirds and scrub jays— to accept our daily food offerings: acorn woodpeckers, red-winged blackbirds, Eurasian collared doves, dark-eyed juncos, spotted towhees, white-breasted nuthatches, black-capped chickadees, oak titmice, and house and golden-crowned sparrows.

In addition to our feeder visitors, we also enjoy watching many other species from our deck. Though seeds aren't included in their diet, robins patrol our yard for worms after springtime rains, with barn swallows sometimes taking insects out of the air above them. We've stationed a concrete birdbath about fifteen yards beyond the railing, next to the tall Douglas-fir. Scrub

Nut hatch.

jays bathe there vigorously, one at a time; western bluebirds often splash around six or eight at a time; and pairs of woodpeckers drink from the bath (but bathe there only infrequently). Meanwhile, red-tailed hawks and turkey vultures circle high above us. Flocks of mallard ducks and Canada geese pass overhead on their way to and from a nearby lake, honking as they go. We share Aldo Leopold's view that it's as important to hear geese as it is to hear Beethoven.

Sometimes we witness true avian drama from our deckside viewing spot—much of it involving hawks. In early spring, the red-tails perform acrobatic courtship flights. Day after day, high in the sky, a male follows a female, diving at her from above, sometimes making contact. Occasionally, the two birds lock talons and fall a long way at great speed before righting themselves. Later, during nesting season, blackbirds and crows will gang up to harass a lone hawk, an activity called "mobbing." The smaller birds, two or three of them, sometimes as many as a dozen, dive at the hawk, often pecking at its back or head in their attempts to drive the predator out of their territory.

In the fall of a recent dry year, with a hawk circling overhead, a covey of valley quail marched in single file, erect as soldiers, out of some brush and unmowed grass toward the birdbath. By the time I looked up at the hawk, it was into its dive, wings laid back, and I knew I had just enough time—a second or two—to stand up, yell, and scatter the quail. But I didn't, for the same reason I don't chase robins out of the yard to protect nightcrawlers: predators have the birthright to hunt their prey.

A few yards above the quail, the hawk braked with outstretched wings and, talons extended, hit the ground hard enough to raise a cloud of brown dust and dry grass. Stubby wings whirring, the quail scattered in all directions. This time the predator's hunt had failed, and it soon returned to the heights.

The incident called to mind a Hemingway line that has it right:

"Life is a hawk in the sky."

One cloudy morning I scattered seeds across the railing, filled the Saint Francis bowl, and deposited bits of a leftover pancake among the seeds. As usual, a scrub jay was the first bird to appear after I rang the dinner bell. Before I had time to put the bell down, it had glided from an oak tree limb and landed on the railing.

"Hello, Blue," I said. "You could be the great-grandchild of an old friend."

Barely an arm's length away, its dark eyes glittered under white eyebrows, blue head cocked to the side.

"What's up?" I asked.

Some readers might bristle at what they see as anthropomorphism, so I should explain that I began talking to birds and animals as a child, and have never stopped. Of course I knew from the beginning that wild creatures couldn't understand what I said; but I believed that, sometimes, they might discern my meaning. I still believe this, and I've known many men and women who talk to wild creatures, including a nationally known conservationist—Oregonian Frank Moore—who takes it a step further and also talks to trees.

The scrub jay turned its back, quickly pecked up four or five pancake pieces, and flew off and out of sight around the house, undoubtedly to choose hiding places for them. Scrub jays, with their episodic-like memories, are believed by some experts to be among the smartest birds alive. Members of the corvid family of songbirds, their brains, relative to their body mass, are the same size as an ape's. They learn from experience, plan ahead, and can precisely memorize as many as two hundred different locations where they've cached food. They also recall which foods are cached at which locations and will return promptly to anything that could spoil. If they suspect that another bird has seen them hide an acorn, or a snail, or a piece of pancake, they move it to a safer place. Both extended families and unrelated groups of jays form such close bonds that they share responsibilities for raising their young and take turns serving as lookouts for predators. A 2012 University of California–Davis study verified the fact that they conduct their own unique funerals, where they screech for as long as half an hour over a dead jay.

When I was a schoolboy in Pennsylvania, a common youthful insult was to call a classmate a birdbrain. One September evening in southern Oregon, a scrub jay proved just how inaccurate that epithet is.

Around a corner and across the yard from our deck is the back door to our garage. In summertime the door stays open all day long; and that evening, while I was splitting and stacking firewood near our irrigation tank, a squawking jay flew within a few feet of me before making a quick turn through the door and into the garage.

I needed a break anyway, so I followed after the jay. A list of the garage's contents is short and simple: a hot-water heater just inside the door, a Ford Focus, a Subaru Impreza, a washing machine and drier against one wall, cross-country skis and poles leaning against another wall, and, underneath a long window on the far side, a workbench scattered with a few random tools and an empty ice chest under the bench. None of these items struck me as something likely to attract or motivate a bird.

The moment I walked through the door, the jay, perched beyond the Ford on the Subaru's roof rack, facing me directly, resumed its squawking. My response was to fall into my old habit of talking to animals and birds.

"Don't you have everything you need right outside?" I asked. "It's beautiful out there." I gestured with my hand. "What could you want in a gloomy garage? One thing you definitely don't want is to get trapped in here all night."

The jay didn't get it. It had fallen silent at my hand gesture, and when I stopped talking, it turned and hopped from the roof rack down onto the workbench behind the Subaru.

"No offense," I said, "but I want you out of here for your own good."

I walked around the front of both cars to get to the workbench, where I found the jay, head tilted to the side, standing between a pipe wrench and a handsaw. When I took a step toward the bird, it hopped backwards. Two more steps, and it flew up to perch on the metal track that houses the garage door pulleys.

"Be reasonable," I said. "Use your head. Scrub jays are supposed to be smart. Brilliant in fact. So think about it and go back outside." When I walked toward the bird, waving both arms, it flapped its wings twice and glided over my head to land back on the workbench.

After I chased the jay back and forth three or four times, it left the metal track to fly over the Subaru and land on the roof of the Ford.

"What's your major malfunction?" I asked politely.

To open the garage door, I walked back around both cars and pressed the control button on the wall between the washing machine and kitchen door. The jay, still stationed on top of the Ford, watched as the door opened. When the door was about halfway up, the bird swooped down, flew outside, and made an abrupt left turn.

So I pressed the button again to close the garage door, and when it was almost all the way down, the jay flew back into the garage behind me, through the back door. With a single loud squawk, it returned to the Subaru roof rack perch.

"Okay," I said. "That's it."

To impart a lesson, I closed the back door, feeling certain that after an hour or two the imprisoned jay would gladly leave and likely never enter the garage again. When I opened the door to get into the kitchen and looked back over my shoulder, the bird began squawking.

"Sorry," I said, "but you asked for it."

I closed the door and the squawking stopped. I stood in the kitchen feeling guilty. What right did I have to play a dirty trick on a bird? I thought about opening both the back door and the garage door to allow the jay to leave whenever it wanted. But before I made up my mind, I heard the unmistakable sound of the garage door going up.

The only possible explanation was that the jay had pecked the control button. By the time I opened the kitchen door, it was gone.

Myna Bird at the Bus Stop

A scrub jay's intelligence, its confidence, its glittering eyes, its size and shape—all remind me of a myna bird that entered my young life in Hawaii. Every morning when the scrub jays feed, I remember both the myna and an old Filipino man named Alejandro.

I was ten years old, waiting impatiently for an early morning bus that would take me to the Outrigger Canoe Club on Waikiki Beach, where I had plans to spend the summer day surfing with friends. As the bus slowed to a stop, I stepped toward the road and saw the fledgling myna bird on its back, head turned to look at me, wings outstretched and entangled in the lush green grass bordering the curb. It didn't struggle as I picked it up. There were no trees nearby, no sign of an adult bird anywhere. The bus door hissed open, and the myna, staring at me, lay damp and nearly weightless against the palm of my right hand.

"Hey, kid, you getting in?" the driver asked.

"I found this baby bird."

"Don't bring 'im in here! Toss the buggah back down! You heard about a bird shortage? You getting in or not?"

I looked at the myna and then at the driver, a bald man with a scowl on his narrow face. With my free left hand I gave him the finger and turned away, and he cursed me as the door closed.

In my cupped hands I carried the myna home. Black eyes glittering, it looked straight at me all the way.

I was a spoiled only child living with my father and mother on the rented second floor of a large house on the corner of Aleo Place and Ferdinand Avenue in upper Manoa Valley. The first floor was occupied by the owners, an elderly couple named Mr. and Mrs. Donalds who owned and operated a prosperous welding company in downtown Honolulu. I call them elderly because, back then, they seemed so to me. Thinking about it now, they were probably in their mid-to-late forties, not much older than my parents. My bedroom was above their living room, and sometimes, while I listened to my radio at low volume late at night, I could hear Mr. Donalds yelling at his wife.

The Donaldses' house and grounds were maintained by an authentically elderly Chinese maid named Lam and an even older Filipino "yard boy" named Alejandro. Alejandro knew about many things, and he helped me care for the myna.

At the edge of the Donaldses' spacious yard was a greenhouse where Mr. Donalds, with Alejandro's help, raised orchids. Within ten minutes of my return with the bird, Alejandro had found a small cardboard box, disposed of the lid, lined the bottom with burlap, and placed the box, with the myna in it, on a low greenhouse shelf. "Always warm in here," he said with a smile. "Young little birds like this got to be warm! Stay here, keiki. I be right back." Alejandro liked teaching me Hawaiian words. Keiki meant "boy."

He jogged downhill toward the house.

The myna lay on its back, wings splayed. I lifted it gently and turned it right side up but, beating its wings weakly, it managed to flop back over.

"You'll be okay," I said. "Alejandro knows what to do."

Moments later, Alejandro, carrying another cardboard box, jogged back up the hill. A small man, smaller even than me, he jogged or ran wherever he went. He worked barefoot and always wore khaki pants cut off below the knees and clean sleeveless white t-shirts.

"Na mea from Lam!" he said as he reached me. "Na mea maikai!"

He lowered the new box to the floor. The na mea maikai—

good things—included two small bowls, some rice, some oatmeal, a hardboiled egg, and an avocado from the tall tree just outside my bedroom window.

As always, Alejandro worked quickly. He filled one of the bowls halfway up with water from a greenhouse spigot and placed it in a corner of the myna's box. After dropping small handfuls of rice and oatmeal into the second bowl, he peeled the egg and avocado, then dropped small bits of egg white and avocado onto the rice and oatmeal. Next, he pulled a switchblade knife from his pants pocket. The long, narrow, shiny blade appeared with a soft click, and he used the point to mash and mix the ingredients together. "Ono!" he said as he placed the food bowl next to the water bowl. "Myna kau! You do like I do," he said. "You do it with kitchen knife. Or a stick from those colored cold things I see you eat sometimes."

"Popsicles?"

"The colored things with sticks."

"Popsicles."

Alejandro used the knife blade to pick up a gob of the food. When he held the food up close to the myna's yellow beak, the bird, one wing beating weakly, turned its head away. When Alejandro tried again, the myna didn't move, but it ignored the offering.

Alejandro wiped both sides of the knife blade against his pant leg. When he pressed the blade back into the handle it made another click. "Got to hana," he said. "Got to work. You know why I work, keiki?"

"To make a living," I said.

"Saving money," Alejandro said. "Pretty soon I die. Got to get my body mailed home, back to Philippines. My kids send it. That's where I want to be, where I came from. With my makuahine a makua. Mom and dad. Kapuna wahine a kapuna kane—grandma and grandpa—too. All buried in Philippines. Cost plenty money to mail me there. I win money at pool halls too. Play all the games. Eight-ball. Rotation. Call shot. Call shot best. No luck in call shot. Save all the money. My people like to shoot pool for money. No Hawaiian word for money. You know why?"

"Because they didn't have any?"

"Had everything they needed without it until haoles came! Didn't need money! Me, I need it now. Got to trim coconut palms today. Listen. We got mynas in Philippines. Got 'em plenty places all over the world I think. Warm places. The mynas, they can talk an' sing like people. Stay here. Try to feed him like I did with a popsicle stick. Pretty soon this myna will eat. Sometime today he will. Feed him every three, four hours. Feed him right before you sleep, right after you get up too, feed him every three, four hours and pretty soon he'll learn how to eat when you gone. Then when he eats when you gone you can give him bugs to eat. Little bugs. Today put some grass in the box. Dump the myna kukai out an' put in new grass an' water every day. Kukai is shit. Tell Mr. Donalds the myna's here in his greenhouse. Tell him to tell you when he turns on sprinklers for his orchids. Ask him to tell you. Then you got to take the myna out till Mr. Donalds turns the sprinklers off. When myna's old enough to fly little bit I build you a cage out of sticks. I know how. When he's big enough you can let him go, let him fly away. Maybe find his kapuna wahine a kapune kane too. If you let him go before he's strong a mongoose gets him. Or you can keep him. Back home in Philippines some people kept mynas. Plenty time I heard mynas talk. Heard 'em sing. Got to be akamai birds to talk and sing like people. Akamai is smart. You know the Hawaiian word for bird?"

"No."

"Manu. Myna bird is manu akamai."

"There's a catamaran at the Outrigger Club named Manu Kai."

"What's a catamaran?"

"A sailboat with two hulls."

Myna bird.

Alejandro smiled. "Manu Kai. Bird of Sea. Pretty damn good name. I got to go trim coconut palms. You stay here."

"Is it a boy or girl myna?"

"With mynas can't tell yet. Can't tell with na keikis. With babies."

I followed Alejandro's instructions. Late in the afternoon of that first day, the myna took food from a popsicle stick. Mr. Donalds assured me he had no reason to water his orchids anytime soon but that before he did water them, he'd tell me.

On the third day the myna began to eat and drink on its own. When a week had passed, I began catching small bugs in the yard and putting them into the box. The myna began hopping onto the back of my hand whenever I reached into the box with more bugs. Perched on my hand, it chirped at me and flapped its wings, then hopped down and started pecking up bugs. Alejandro explained that young birds flap their wings for exercise because soon they will fly, and that now it was time for him to build a big stick cage.

Early the next morning, as I was looking out my bedroom window, Alejandro appeared from behind the high hedge that bordered Aleo Place. He came down the driveway at a jog, carrying the cage. I hurried downstairs and met him in the lower yard, underneath the avocado tree. The solidly built cage was about two feet wide and two feet high. Both the floor and ceiling were rattan, and the koa sticks that formed the walls and ceiling were lashed together with twine. Three of the vertical wall sticks had short protruding limbs meant to serve as perches.

"What you think?" Alejandro asked me with a smile. "Here. Take um. No cage door. Roof lifts off."

I could see that he was proud of the cage he'd built. I took it and lifted it up and down, then turned it around slowly to examine all four sides. I set the cage on the ground and lifted the roof off and set it back down. "It's great!" I exclaimed. "Thanks!"

"Welcome. That myna be ready fly away in two weeks. Maybe even not so long. Ready to live on own soon. It's a boy bird. You going to let him go? You going to keep him? What you think?"

"I'd kind of like to keep him. But I'm not sure."

"Why you want to keep him?"

"I like him. I could teach him to talk." I'd thought a lot about it. I wanted to teach the myna to swear, to say things I wasn't supposed to say and, with luck, say them to people I wasn't supposed to say them to. If anyone complained about his language, I'd lie and say I hadn't taught him the bad words, he'd somehow picked them up on his own. "I could keep the cage up in my room, hang it from the ceiling. What would you do?"

"What I would do? Let him go. But you found him. You decide. You the boss."

I felt embarrassed when Alejandro called me the boss.

But I didn't have to make a decision. When we took the cage into the greenhouse, we found the myna dead. Sometime during the night, Mr. Donalds had turned on the sprinklers and left them on for a long time. The saturated cardboard box had collapsed. When Alejandro lifted off the lid, the myna lay on his side on matted wet grass, his small bright dead eyes staring at nothing. I picked him up and held him as I had at the bus stop, cold and wet in the palm of my hand.

"Don't cry," Alejandro said.

"I can't help it."

"Doesn't change things. Doesn't help."

"I can't help it though."

We buried the myna in his ruined box, far across the yard from the greenhouse. Alejandro dug the hole about two feet deep.

"No more crying," he said.

Alejandro was crying too, for me, tears streaming down his furrowed cheeks.

About two months after the myna died, Alejandro was killed in a knife fight. His body was discovered by garbage men in the early morning, in a downtown Honolulu alley around the corner from a pool hall.

No one ever found out who had killed Alejandro, or why. When I asked Mr. Donalds, he didn't know—and didn't seem to care whether or not Alejandro's body had been shipped back to the Philippines.

I lived in Hawaii for seven more years and spent much of my free time on Oahu's beaches: Waikiki, Makapuu, Sand Beach, Makaha, Laie. No matter where I was or what I was doing—surfing, bodysurfing, spearing fish, paddling a canoe—I looked for frigate birds (iwa in Hawaiian) and watched them closely. A beach boy had taught me about them. Large birds with dark plumage and forked tails, they circle over deep blue water searching the surface for fish or squid. Their feathers aren't waterproof, so they can't land on water, but with their six-foot wingspans and opportunistic knowledge of trade winds and thermal updrafts, they can stay aloft for weeks at a time. To me they represented freedom. They made me feel like a dog on a leash, or a goldfish in a bowl, and I wanted what they had.

Frigate bird.

Elegant Complexity

A titmouse took a single seed from the railing, sailed away immediately, returned within seconds for another seed, and then sailed off again. A nuthatch replaced the titmouse, also to take one seed; it then climbed up the wooden stanchion supporting the deck's slatted roof. Once it reached the roof, it flew off in the same direction the titmouse had taken. Next a collared dove arrived, bringing to mind the first pair of that species Hilde and I had ever seen.

On a lightly clouded October morning in 2015, two pale gray birds the color of the sky glided across the yard. One landed on the railing and the other on the edge of the St. Francis bowl. After looking us over briefly, they began quickly pecking up seeds. It was clear that these were doves but that they were larger, more heavily built, and too light-colored to be mourning doves, the species native to southern Oregon.

Thanks to the internet, within minutes we'd identified the newcomers as Eurasian collared doves, so named because of the black half-collar at the nape of their necks. Collared doves are handsome if not spectacular creatures. Their black bills, dark eyes, smoothly feathered gray bodies, and white tail feathers exemplify what the Japanese call shibui—elegant simplicity.

Until the end of the nineteenth century, collared doves were found only in the Middle East, ranging from Turkey eastward to China and south through India. During the twentieth century, their range expanded to include most of Europe—from Norway south—and the Canary Islands and northern Africa. In 1974,

Collared dove.

a few dozen doves escaped captivity in the Bahamas, and from there the birds spread first to Florida, then gradually northward and westward. Today, nearly every state has a collared dove population.

During the years since the first pair visited our feeder in Ashland, their local numbers have rapidly increased. Now, there are people in our neighborhood who want to see them—along with all other invasive species—eliminated.

Many invasive species do, of course, inflict serious ecological damage. Feral swine, descendants of escaped or released pigs, now spread diseases to people and animals (among their many other ecologically destructive impacts) on every continent except Antarctica. Brown marmorated stink bugs, native to east Asia, are now wreaking agricultural havoc—and infesting people's homes—across the United States. Warm water bass released into streams by irresponsible anglers displace native trout, and mongooses native to India have decimated Hawaii's endemic bird population.

But other invasive species do no harm at all, including the beautiful ring-necked pheasant (also native to Asia) and yes, the Eurasian collared dove, a symbol of peace.

While Hilde and I admired the pair of collared doves, we agreed that their personalities were as impressive as their unassuming beauty. We respected the way they stood their ground in the face of bullying acorn woodpeckers and then, when the woodpeckers left, shared space with tiny sparrows.

Watching these doves with international lineage lifted our spirits, and not even the prospect that an "America First" xenophobe was closing in on his party's nomination as its presidential candidate could ruin our good moods that morning. And the doves were only one of many multicultural elements that were enriching our day. The millet seeds the doves and sparrows were feeding on probably originated in Africa, and as we watched the birds we were enjoying delicious Costa Rican coffee. Down a hill and across the road was a pasture where six horses grazed, two of them a beautiful species that originated on the Arabian Peninsula. A couple up the road from us raises Barbados Blackbelly sheep—which themselves have African and European ancestry. On my mother's side, I'm descended from a Mohawk war chief; and my father's ancestors came from northern Germany and Ireland. I grew up in Hawaii before it became a state and married Hilde in Bavaria, where her family has lived for centuries. After our mid-morning walk, we were looking forward to lunch at an excellent local Mexican restaurant.

An enjoyable life can be as elegantly complex as that.

Hunting and Killing

> Killing has a place in hunting, if only a small one. I see it as a rite, a sacrifice, an acknowledgement of the sport's origin that gives meaning to what has gone before. But never as an end in itself.
>
> —Roderick Haig-Brown, *Measure of the Year: Reflections on Home, Family, and a Life Fully Lived*

Four or five times a week, starting from home, Hilde and I take out-and-back walks along various rural roads and forest trails. One of our routes takes us past a fenced quarter-acre chicken enclosure on a small farm, and when we go that way, we take along a sack of feed: popcorn kernels that didn't pop, sunflower seeds, and dried corn. The chickens see us coming from a long way off, and by the time we reach their fence at least three dozen are jammed against the wire, hens clucking, roosters crowing loudly.

A few seconds after we toss the first handful through the wire, latecomers rush out of the coop, wings flapping, running as fast as they can go to join the feeding frenzy. Altogether there are maybe forty birds, a single white turkey among them. The turkey, we learned from the couple who own the farm, was purchased to become Thanksgiving dinner, but their young son and daughter wouldn't allow it.

Most humans underestimate the intelligence and resourcefulness of chickens, but research has proved beyond any doubt that they are highly intelligent birds with instincts much like those of their jungle fowl ancestors. Though it sounds like mere "clucking" to us, chickens utilize dozens of vocalizations to communicate information about nesting, breeding, mating, feeding, contentment, and possible distress or danger. Each flock establishes a hierarchy, or pecking order, with a dominant rooster charged with protecting the chicks and hens. Dominant and submissive hens separate themselves into distinct groups. Submissive roosters are often clever enough to divert the dominant male's attention and find a way to mate with a compliant hen. A notable finding in a 2011 University of Bristol study of chickens is that they remember what they've learned through trial and error, and they apply their knowledge to future situations.

It's clear that few of us know or care much about any of this, however. Every year, about nine billion chickens in the US and as many as fifty billion globally are slaughtered for food; and before suffering gruesome deaths, very nearly all of them exist in horrendous conditions.

Years ago I met and briefly knew a man who made his living guiding hunters and anglers, and who told me how he'd exorcised his frustration and disgust with the treatment chickens endure. At two a.m. on his way home from a fishing trip, he passed an egg farm that he'd seen before, but only during daylight hours. With no moon in the sky and no vehicles in sight, he parked alongside the road, took a tire iron out of the trunk, and carried it to the nearest building. Once he'd disabled the lock, the door slid open easily on lubricated rollers.

Inside the egg farm, under dim lighting, he saw long rows of wire cages stretching the length of the building, white hens crammed into every cage. To prevent the hens from injuring one another their beaks had been burned off, without painkillers, soon after they hatched. The ammonia stench of urine and feces was intense. As the hens clucked, he pried open the first cage with the tire iron. He worked his way along using the tire iron as a club. As hens scurried out of their cages, he clobbered their heads. They fluttered and squawked, and blood squirted and splashed as—these were his words—"I rescued as many of them as I could from their bleak existence."

Having been an upland bird hunter for much of my life, I'm well aware that, as Americans separate themselves further and further from the natural world in the twenty-first century, wholesale condemnation of hunting and hunters by those who don't themselves engage in the practice is also on the rise. On his HBO television show *Real Time* several years ago, host Bill Maher dismissed hunters as "sadists who enjoy murdering chipmunks." I think that's a very heavy-handed description, and I also think that those of us who do eat meat should at least occasionally be required to kill our own. Why should a stranger do it for us, and another stranger package it in plastic? Leo Tolstoy, also at one time an upland bird hunter (though later in life a vegetarian), is known to have offered houseguests who wanted meat a live chicken and a hatchet.

All of this leads me to the conclusion that there are innumerable human activities for which blanket generalizations are useless. An extreme example is the fact that Adolph Hitler became a vegetarian during the period of his life when he was waging world war and murdering millions of innocent people. So vegetarianism isn't necessarily a virtue, and neither is ethical hunting a vice.

For better or worse, I adopted a vegetarian diet for a period of about three years, and during that time I gave up hunting. When I went back to eating meat, I also started hunting again, and I enjoyed it. Until about eleven thousand years ago, all humans were hunter-gatherers. In his esteemed 2011 book *Sapiens, A Brief History of Humankind,* Yuval Noah Harari concludes that hunter-gatherers were likely the happiest human beings who ever lived. In the framework of evolutionary history, eleven thousand years is a very short time; and I understand that, for better or worse, the desire to hunt is written in my blood. I also simply prefer real meat, wild meat, to the often contaminated products found in supermarkets.

But any examination of hunting must begin with the fundamental fact that true hunting and opportunistic killing (aka vain macho bloodlust) are very different things. By way of illustration, I offer here portraits of two men who represent the two extremes. The first, a friend of mine named Miller, hunted only mountain quail, arguably the most challenging North American game bird. The bird earned its name by living in the West Coast's steep, high-elevation terrain, usually in forests of oak, pine, and fir, often near creeks where thick brush provides heavy cover.

I hunted with Miller in the isolated area he favored, a vast, grassy valley far from any trace of civilization and a two-hour uphill walk from anywhere you can leave your car. A healthy creek courses through the valley, and quail often shelter in willow thickets and stands of buckbrush near the water. Once they are flushed from cover, the birds tend to fly up the steep surrounding mountainsides into old-growth forest. Chasing after them is exhausting work. Miller calculated that he covered at least six miles of rugged country for every quail he took home. He also reckoned that by breaking up coveys when he hunted—chasing small groups of birds into country that was new to them, and where they then stayed and bred—he more than doubled the valley's mountain quail population. There were two large coveys when he discovered his hunting spot, and a few years later there were five.

Unlike my friend Miller, I also pursued other species of upland birds in my hunting days, but a lot of things made mountain quail my favorite both to hunt and to admire: their beauty, their elusiveness, their unpredictability, and, most of all, the fact that because of the rugged country they inhabit, they're the least hunted and least seen game bird in America.

Once, from a distance, I watched a bobcat sneaking up on a feeding quail covey in the gray light of early morning. Just as

Mountain quail.

the cat appeared ready to pounce, the birds flushed en masse and then scattered, dark blurs that curved through the trees and quickly vanished. The cat stood looking after them, seemingly bewildered, a feeling I knew well.

Out hiking, I watched a pair of quail lure a coyote away from a nest full of eggs beneath a pine tree. Two weeks later I checked that nest, and it held eighteen or twenty tiny chicks that flew down a steep slope on inch-long wings. Now that I no longer visit mountain quail country, I like knowing that the birds are there, and that unlike many wildlife species, they'll remain there in healthy numbers long after I die.

In the early 1880s, ring-necked pheasants—which happen to be cousins of the chickens discussed earlier in this chapter—were shipped from Shanghai to Oregon and released on the lower Columbia River and in the Willamette Valley. Like collared doves, this species thrived and quickly spread through Oregon and Washington. Today there are forty states, from Pennsylvania to Hawaii, that have pheasant populations, and the spectacularly beautiful roosters are popular game birds wherever they exist.

A self-styled hunter, a medical doctor I'll call James, enjoyed shooting these birds, and he once invited me to accompany him to his favorite place to engage in the sport. It turned out to be a ten-acre stubble field with a 1950s ranch-style house near its center. We parked in a paved lot near the house and walked into a makeshift office reeking of cigarette smoke. A smiling man, dressed up as a cowboy and sitting behind a cluttered desk, greeted James and assured him that everything would be ready in ten or fifteen minutes.

So James and I sat on an uncomfortable couch to wait, making small talk. Behind our host was a large window, and I watched a shiny pickup truck roll across the field and stop no more than a hundred yards from the house. A young man, also masquerading as a cowboy, climbed out and, one by one, lifted pheasants from a large wooden crate in the truck bed. Holding each bird upside down by the legs, he swung it around in fast circles for several seconds as he walked, then dropped it into the stubble. A black Lab sat next to the truck, watching. I counted twenty dizzy and disoriented pheasants, all deposited on less than two acres of ground. I remembered an appalling account I'd read of former Vice President Dick Cheney bragging to friends about shooting seventy-five pheasants in a single afternoon. At the time I'd wondered how such a thing could be possible. Now I understood.

Our host told us it was time to hunt. The fat rooster pheasants, all without tails and having spent their entire lives crammed into cages, could barely lift themselves off the ground. James began shooting them, while I purposely missed two birds and then quit.

It took no more than half an hour for James to kill all twenty pheasants. The pair of fake cowboys stood together next to the pickup truck while the Lab retrieved the dead and struggling birds, which were then stuffed into a burlap sack.

All I wanted to do was leave. But first, back inside the office, we had to wait until the pheasants had been run through what the host called "a plucking machine." While that was happening, James handed over a five-hundred-dollar check. As we walked back to the car, the burlap sack slung over James's shoulder, a pair of turkey vultures circled over the stubble field, possibly hoping to spot a bird or two the Lab had missed.

"Sorry you didn't care for it much," James said with a smile. "But that's my idea of fun!"

"Do you come here often?"

"A few times a year. Come on back with me another time. Maybe you'll learn to like it!"

I'd much prefer finding myself at Tolstoy's estate, a chicken in one hand and a hatchet in the other.

Tiny Drop of Bright Red Blood

On a grouse-hunting day with my German shorthair Otto, I learned that the changes people experience can be far more abrupt and less predictable than seasons of the year.

During the drive up the north slope of Grizzly Peak, a covey of mountain quail crossed the gravel road in front of us. Visible in silhouette in the early morning light, at least a dozen birds marched along in quick-legged single file. The moment I slowed to let them pass, Otto saw them. His ears cocked forward, and he whined, then howled, then pawed at the window.

"Otto! No!"

He stopped pawing but, quivering with excitement, kept whining until the last of the birds had disappeared into cover. Fifteen minutes later, and a thousand feet higher, we parked. I knew that it might be too early to find blue grouse out feeding; but Otto didn't know, so for half an hour, I let him hunt at his own pace to work off some excess energy.

By the time we'd worked around to Grizzly's eastern slope, the sun was well into the sky. Otto's initial burst of vigor had dissipated, and I'd warmed with the morning.

"Look around! Stay close now!" (No, dogs don't know any more English than wild birds and other animals do. These were essential commands he'd been carefully trained to obey.)

We slowly circled a huge patch of elderberries surrounded by Douglas-firs. Then I worked my way through the berry bushes, Otto between ten and twenty yards out ahead. In an hour we'd combed the entire patch, the dog's stubby tail wagging constantly but never becoming the blur that would have meant we were near a bird.

Up a slope beyond the fir trees was a spring. If the grouse weren't feeding yet, they might be getting water. The climb was long and steep, and before we reached the spring I was sweating. I took my jacket off and knotted the sleeves around my waist.

Water oozed from the mountainside and spread as it descended through the knee-high green grass growing in the shade of trees. Shortly after starting off through the grass, Otto hit the scent. Nose twitching, he crept forward in search of the strong channel of scent that would lead to a bird. My boots sank into wet, porous earth as I followed.

"Stay close," I whispered.

Just as I spoke, Otto froze on point, bent right leg poised, head and neck stretched forward—still as a statue except for the twitching nose. When I stopped beside him, his brown eyes moved to mine as if checking to make sure I was ready.

I thought I was. For my first bird, I'd decided to take whatever shot presented itself. After that, I'd pass up any easy chances.

Another step forward and a grouse exploded out of the grass a yard from Otto's nose and flew straight away at eye level, the easiest shot there is.

I had the gun up, my cheek pressed against the stock, the bead at the end of the barrel squarely on target. The grouse was twenty-five yards out when I pulled the trigger. Nothing happened. Though I'd made such shots dozens of times before, this time I'd somehow neglected to release the safety. By the time I'd done that, the grouse was forty yards out with the gun no longer on it. When I had the grouse in my sights again, it was more than sixty yards away and into the trees. That was much too far, but—stupidly, uselessly—I fired anyway, wasting both barrels.

I cursed myself for fouling up such a simple shot, and for compounding my incompetence by trying one that was impossible. As I broke open the gun to eject the spent shells, another grouse burst out of the grass a yard from where the first one had emerged. I grabbed two shells from my vest pocket, dropped one, jammed the other into the gun, and slammed it shut. With the grouse still in reasonable range I shouldered the stock, aimed, pulled the trigger, and heard a click. In my haste I'd shoved the single shell into the upper chamber, but on over-and-under shotguns the lower barrel fires first. I jerked the trigger again in frustrated rage and missed the grouse.

When a third grouse burst out of the grass behind me, I spun around and instinctively raised the gun again before realizing it was empty.

Even in a long day, a grouse hunter is lucky to get one chance as easy as the three I'd ruined in the space of fifteen seconds. Still, I wanted one more chance, to redeem myself. But Otto and I hunted a long loop back toward the car without flushing another bird.

I felt like a failure because of the mistakes I'd made, and like a fool for allowing it to bother me the way it had. Then, a minute or two short of the car, a grouse flushed from underneath a ponderosa pine about ten yards up a steep slope to my left. Without thinking, I spun and fired. Forty yards out I saw a puff of feathers. The grouse was surely dead before it began to fall. Otto, who had heard the flush, picked the bird up seconds after it thudded onto the pine-needle-covered forest floor. He brought it to hand.

I felt no elation when I took the bird from him. Now that I had it, what I'd wanted so badly seemed meaningless. I certainly didn't see the dead grouse as redemption. It wasn't much of a trophy, either. I couldn't even think of it as a meal. I held it, soft-feathered in my hand, warm and limp, a tiny drop of bright red blood at the tip of its beak—and I knew I was through with regarding killing as my hunting end-game.

I'd questioned the ethos of hunting to kill before, as all reasonable hunters surely have. My opinion had always been, and still is, that there are at least as many compelling arguments in favor of this method of securing food—if responsibly practiced—as there are against it.

But something had changed in me. It connected with the dismay I'd felt when I recognized the shallowness of my desire to prove myself, to myself, through the act of killing. I'd made or missed all varieties of shots in many places over many years. So why continue? Had I done enough shooting?

On the way down Grizzly, Otto asleep on the seat beside me, I wondered about our morning. I decided I was as glad I'd messed up my chances on the first three grouse as I was sorry about succeeding with the last one. A hunter, a dog, and an upland bird are as alive as they can ever be at the moment of that sudden, powerful flush from cover. It's likely that only hunters will know what I'm getting at here.

A Logging Road Down a Mountainside

> I come home with a chicken or
> a rabbit and sit up
> singing all night with my friends.
> It's baroque, my life, and
> I tell it on the mountain.
>
> I wouldn't trade it for yours.
>
> —William Stafford, "Coyote"

Our reddish, long-haired cat trotted across the lawn and then up the three wooden steps onto the deck. At age fifteen, Dingbat remains healthy and energetic, and throughout his life he's understood that the birds we feed are off limits. He ignores them, and they ignore him, except for a single scrub jay with either a grudge or a sense of humor, or both.

The jay loves to taunt the cat. When Dingbat ambles across the yard and the jay is anywhere close enough to see him, it sails down and lands three or four feet away from the cat, facing him directly. Then, bobbing its head up and down, it squawks at full volume, directly in Dingbat's face. For five or ten minutes, sometimes longer, wherever Dingbat goes, the jay maintains the distance between them, walking forward or backing up, squawking relentlessly. It's clear that the bird enjoys harassing the cat—and misses this pastime on days when Dingbat stays inside, most often curled up asleep on a dining room chair. When that happens, the jay likes to perch on the arm of a deck chair, squawking at the cat through the glass door at a distance of six or eight feet. The jay flies off when Dingbat wakes up, hops off the chair, stretches, and heads to his food dish in the kitchen.

Every time I witness this routine, Dingbat's brother Whitey comes to mind.

Looking eastward from our deck at the valley floor, we can see horses, cattle, sheep, goats, and peacocks in fenced pastures—interspersed in recent years with carefully tended marijuana and hemp grows. As they've been doing for tens of thousands of years, coyotes come down from the mountains at night to catch what they can. Late at night, we sometimes hear them yipping and howling, and occasionally, just after morning's first light, we spot one or two of them prowling the pastures and farmyards.

A few months ago, a coyote killed and devoured Whitey. Hilde discovered what was left of the cat—little more than a head and tail and four legs—under a pine tree close to our storage shed. I buried him nearby.

It must have been the same coyote that came back a few days later to try for Dingbat. When I walked out our back door that morning to split some of the firewood logs stacked against the shed, a brief movement caught my eye, a quick flash of darkness behind a shrub. I stopped, looked hard, saw nothing; and then, when I took a single step toward the shrub, a coyote sprang from its cover, landed on all fours with its big ears cocked forward, and turned its black-nosed, narrow-snouted head to stare at me with bright yellow eyes. This was a healthy, handsome animal, with thick brown fur tinged with black and a bushy tail held high, but I had no more than a second to admire it.

The coyote sprinted back behind the shed with the kind of speed that made it seem to simply vanish. I had time to take two steps toward the shed before it reappeared after coming up against our nearby next-door neighbor's tall wooden fence. This time it didn't pause to look me over. Our own four-foot-high wire fence separates us from the neighbor far down the hill, and, after a sharp right pivot, the coyote, at least six feet from the fence, jumped it with no apparent effort, easily clearing the wire. By the time I reached the fence a few seconds later, the animal was out of sight in the brushy cover a hundred yards away.

Ever since my close encounter with that coyote, Hilde and I have been arguing about it. She says she'd kill the coyote if she could, to protect Dingbat. I care about Dingbat too, and we do our best to keep him out of harm's way. But I don't believe in using leg-hold traps or canisters of cyanide or guns—or anything else—against coyotes.

My respect for coyotes—or call it love—dates back to a night many years ago when Hilde and I cross-country skied a logging road down a mountainside under a full moon. Cross-country skis through powder snow make an eerie, muted hissing sound; and I think it was that sound, along with the moon, that started the coyotes howling. A pack of them followed us down the mountain. One would bark, then yip, then produce a long, drawn-out howl, the note rising shrilly as the volume increased. The louder the howl became, the closer it seemed, and when the animals joined in chorus, they seemed very close indeed.

We looked back often on our descent, but of course we never saw one. They followed us all the way to our car, and it wasn't until the skis had been lashed to the roof rack that they finally fell silent. No sound on earth—except perhaps a wolf's howl—could be wilder, freer, more beautiful than what we heard that winter night.

Thoreau wrote in his essay "Walking" that "in wildness is the preservation of the world," and though I don't know exactly what that meant to him, I know what it means to me. To my mind, wild birds and animals are superior to the domestic species that people breed and train and to the creatures we slaughter to eat. Superior in the sense that they live exactly where and how they were meant to live—and have no way of knowing that they won't exist exactly as they are forever.

Stiff, Sore, Tired, Dirty

Self-reliance is not the same thing as self-interest.
—Lauren Groff, "Waiting for the End of the World"

I wanted to try, for a week, to come as close as I could get to living wild.

On a mid-October day, I parked in a clearing several yards off a rural two-lane road, followed a narrow trail through a stand of old-growth Douglas-firs and cedars, found a creek at the end of the trail, and hiked up it. I wore a wide-brimmed fishing hat, a sweatshirt, jeans, and a well-worn pair of Nikes, with a warm jacket knotted around my waist. I carried a single-shot 20-gauge shotgun and had a hunting knife and hatchet in my belt. In my pocket were a dozen matches I'd waterproofed by dipping the heads in hot wax, two shotgun shells, ten feet of six-pound-test fishing line, and two barbless hooks embedded in a wine bottle cork.

The creek, lined with alders and maples, ran wild and lovely, flowing clear among gray, mossy boulders. Fallen leaves from the hardwoods lay thick along the banks and moved in the current to collect in eddies. In a roadless and uninhabited expanse of country, the creek water would be uncontaminated with chemicals or waste.

Utilizing the extra eyelids that enable it to see underwater and the scales that plug its nostrils when it dives, a water ouzel (American dipper) at a small pool vanished into the depths to feed on nymphs and larvae. More ouzels appeared as I worked my way upstream, and leaves fell in bright shafts of sunlight slanting

Water ouzel.

through the trees. But there wasn't much sunlight—the bigleaf maples and alders were thick, as were the firs and cedars—and before I'd travelled a quarter mile I was worried. There'd been rain in September and early October, and though the skies had been clear for several days, the woods were sodden. My shoes and pant legs were soaked, and I could see my breath when I exhaled. Dry kindling might be hard to find.

Up ahead I heard what I knew to be a pileated woodpecker drumming loudly against a tree. Pileateds, at least twice the size of the acorn woodpeckers that feed in our back yard, live deep in forests and are rarely seen. I was lucky enough to spot this one at once, near the top of a tall, dead Douglas-fir, its oversized crest brilliant red in the sunlight, its long, powerful beak moving in a blur against the gray wood of the old tree, likely excavating insects.

I stood and watched, reminiscing about the last pileated I'd had a good look at while running on a logging road in the Ashland watershed on a warm day in May three or four decades ago.

That bird had been high in a dead fir as well, also uncovering insects, and I'd watched it at work as I ran. But then I'd come to a sudden dead stop, my way forward having been blocked by a big black bear and her two cubs. I'd have seen the bears sooner if I hadn't been distracted by the woodpecker overhead. As it was, the bears and I were separated by no more than six feet of logging road.

The mother stood to the left of her cubs. All three animals were staring at me. Heart pounding, arms and legs gone numb, I'd found myself staring back at the mother, my mind racing. I knew that mother bears with cubs were said to be very dangerous, and I'd heard and read advice about how to handle chance confrontations with both bears and cougars. With one of these animals, it was supposedly best to raise your arms to appear big, and to scream loudly; but with the other, walking slowly away was the best strategy. With one of them it was best to make eye contact; but with the other, eye contact was a mistake. I couldn't remember which of the two animals any of this advice applied to. My brain at that point was as numb as my arms and legs, and I made what I'd later recall was the wrong choice when I stared straight into the large, dark eyes of the mother bear.

With all four of us frozen in place, I'd started talking. I'd made a conscious effort to sound calm, even friendly, but had no idea whether or not I was succeeding in that. "I couldn't hurt you if I wanted to," I'd said. "You must understand that. And of course I wouldn't want to. But I don't quite know what to do now. This is your country out here. Those are damn fine-looking cubs you've got there. I haven't ever seen nicer-looking bear cubs anytime, anywhere, and that's the honest truth." My mouth was so dry I'd had to clear my throat. When I did, the mother bear blinked. I think I blinked too. There was no other movement by any of us. "Please give me a break," I'd said. "I'd truly appreciate it."

I'd run out of things to say. The standoff continued for I don't know how long. I couldn't read the mother bear's eyes. I saw no fear, and I didn't think I saw anger either. After a period of time that felt much longer than it actually was, she finally made up her mind. Still staring at me, she reached out a paw and shoved one cub off the downhill side of the road. Then she did the same to the other, and then she followed after them, ambling away.

I'd watched the three of them until they were more than twenty

Pileated woodpecker.

yards away, and by then I had recovered my ability to run. I'd realized that the pileated woodpecker was still drumming.

My first priority today was finding a back-up shelter, a dry place to retreat to if it rained. Hiking along the creek was slow going, but after a couple of miles and an hour or so, I discovered what I wanted. High winter water had carved a depression four or five feet deep into the creek's west bank, forming what amounted to a small cave. The cave's floor was fairly flat, if rocky; and its roof, thickly laced with roots, appeared to be stable. A few yards below the depression, a cedar had fallen across the stream and driftwood had collected behind it, the logjam creating a pool at least four feet deep where several small trout were holding, dark-backed and clearly visible against the bedrock bottom.

The trout made me want to fish, but my next priority was to find a decent location for a campsite and a fire. I climbed the steep bank, looking for a clearing where the sun had dried some brush. Already I was lonely, wishing I'd brought Luke, our six-month-old golden retriever.

Though it didn't please me to admit this to myself, I was also vaguely anxious. For the first time in my life, nobody—including me—knew exactly where I was. I'd told Hilde the general area

I'd be in, but if it came to any sort of emergency, a search party would be lucky to find me by Christmas.

Soon the strain of the climb wiped all such thoughts away. Blazing a tree trunk every forty or fifty yards with my hatchet—I wanted to be able to get back to my cave in a hurry in case of inclement weather—I climbed about a thousand feet in half an hour. When Steller's jays scolded from tree branches overhead, I wondered if the hatchet noise had set them off. In any case, the sound of familiar birds was reassuring. Then a pair of ravens glided in to land side by side on the low branch of a Douglas-fir. I was glad to see them and figured that the scolding jays weren't.

Sweat was pouring off me by the time I hit a narrow game trail that continued upward through the trees. It was so steep here that even the deer used switchbacks. I hadn't gone far before I came across a dead doe, a recent kill. Both hindquarters had been gnawed away, along with the stomach all the way to the ribs. It had been either a cougar or coyotes, or both. Not far ahead of me the jays were scolding louder than ever, and now it wasn't reassuring. Whatever had killed the doe could be nearby.

I wrote off my reaction as irrational fear. After another half hour of climbing, my quadriceps feeling the strain, I saw that some of the big firs bore black scars from an old wildfire. One large tree had come down in a storm, its huge network of roots a few yards off the game trail on the downhill side. Just beyond that deadfall, fire had burned through a four-or-five-acre clearing now overgrown with brush, including a number of elderberry bushes. I could eat the berries, and I knew that grouse would feed there too. Between one elderberry bush and the fire-scarred trees at the forest's border were a few feet of level ground at the base of an outcropping of smooth gray rock—a suitable place to build a fire, sleep, and, as best I could figure, catch early morning sunlight.

I lay the shotgun, the shells, my jacket, and my box of matches at the base of the outcropping, then searched the area for kindling. A skein of geese passed by so high in the sky that I could barely hear their honking, and higher yet were dozens of circling turkey vultures, apparently gathering to migrate south.

In twenty minutes I'd collected a supply of dry sticks that would last me three or four days. As I gathered the kindling, I noticed small grasshoppers clinging to twigs and settled on the rocky earth itself, lethargic now in the cool fall weather. I swatted about a dozen of them with my hat, killing them without crushing them, and slid them carefully into the same pocket that held the hooks and monofilament line.

Now I was more eager than ever to fish. First, though, I made three trips down the slope to the fallen fir tree, where I hacked thick chunks of dried bark from its underside and carried them back to stack by the kindling. When I finally started down to the creek to catch my dinner, I felt pleasantly secure, having made my temporary home.

But when I passed the dead doe, a wave of fear went through me. I stopped by the carcass and looked behind me, then all around. It was afternoon now, and dark in the shade of the forest. All I saw were trees. The Steller's jays were silent.

It's surprising how little effort and time it takes to get back down a hill that was a test to climb. As I drank the creek's cold, sweet water, I calculated there were a good two hours of daylight left, which meant I had up to an hour to fish.

I didn't actually need that much time but used it anyway, which turned out to be a mistake. With a hook turle-knotted to the end of my coiled ten-foot line, I made my way upstream, sneaking up on each small pool. The pools were separated by stretches where the creek flowed only inches deep between the gray boulders. Most pools were no more than three or four feet across and two feet deep, while a very few—those formed behind logjams or beneath falls—were three times as wide and up to six feet deep. These larger pools held the most and biggest trout, and I felt certain that they had never been fished for.

Each time I dropped my grasshopper-laden line onto the surface, several trout shot up at the bait; it was merely a question of which one would reach the grasshopper first. I hooked two seven-inchers in the first pool I tried. Even when I came out from behind a boulder and stood over the pool in plain sight, the remaining trout attacked again and again when I dropped the bait onto the water. I pulled it away before they could reach it, but when I dropped it back they returned, the smallest fish rising a dozen times or more before they tired of the game. In all, I explored some two dozen pools after my early catches, either releasing the trout I hooked or pulling the bait away before they could take it.

I saw the occasional ouzel all the way along, their dark, long-legged bodies bobbing up and down as they perched on streamside rocks or midstream boulders, their eyes flashing white as they blinked while issuing their high-pitched calls. As I fished, a flock of band-tailed pigeons, perhaps a dozen birds, landed on two low limbs of a dead fir and perched there watching me. The largest North American pigeon species, band-tails are also the closest genetic relative of passenger pigeons, which probably were once the planet's most abundant bird—numbering in the billions—but have been extinct since 1914, when the last one, named Martha, died in the Cincinnati Zoo. Now, due primarily to logging, the band-tail populations are also shrinking at an alarming rate; this was the first flock I'd seen in years.

I kept thinking I'd turn back after one more pool, make my climb, start a fire, and cook my dinner. Invariably, though, the next pool upstream looked promising—and the next, and the one after that. Finally, I came to a pool at the base of a three-foot waterfall that really was the best one yet—about fifteen feet long, ten feet across, and at least eight feet deep, with a gravel-covered bottom and a submerged bedrock ledge on its far side. I felt certain that at least one big trout had to be holding somewhere underneath that ledge.

I climbed onto a boulder to try to toss a grasshopper far enough to reach the ledge. The hopper landed where I wanted it to, and the big trout—at least twelve inches, maybe fourteen—came out of the shadows and started up.

But in straining to make the long toss, I leaned so far forward that I lost my balance. Swaying there atop the rounded boulder, right arm flailing while my left hand gripped the line, I watched the trout rise through water so clear it appeared to be swimming through air. But it was indeed water—and ice cold, as I discovered when I fell face forward into the pool.

It was a shock. This heavily shaded creek was fed by early snowmelt from the high country, and the water temperature must have been around forty-five degrees. When I clambered out of the pool I was gasping for breath and shivering. I still gripped the line in my hand, but I hadn't hooked the trout.

Soaked, I climbed back up the mountainside, moving at least twice as fast as I had the first time. At one point I thought I might be lost. When I reached the bend where I thought I'd seen the dead doe, it was gone. Then I saw blood stains where the carcass had been, and I could see where it had been dragged away, uphill into the trees. That meant I was likely sharing the area with a cougar.

Despite the effort of the climb, I was still cold when I reached my clearing.

Handling the flame carefully, I managed to start a fire with my first match, then carefully added progressively larger sticks of kindling, and finally wedged a slab of bark against the rock outcropping, directly over the small blaze. After a minute or two the bark began to smoke, then sputter; and finally the edges burst into orange flame.

By the time the fire was blazing, night had fallen. I squatted, naked except for my jacket, drying my clothes from the inside out: underwear and socks first, then jeans and sweatshirt, then my hat, finally my shoes. After wringing each of these things out as best I could, I held them over the fire on sticks. The nylon running shoes dried quickly, but everything else—especially the sweatshirt—took a long time, and as the clothing steamed there was nothing to do but think. As I'd learn through the following days and nights, there's no way to avoid thinking when you're truly all alone. When one's immediate needs are satisfied—and perhaps some future needs as well—distractions are few.

When I was dressed again, including my jacket, I roasted my trout, holding them over the fire on one of my clothes-drying sticks. As I ate the fish and spit out the bones, I thought about the cougar. I'd heard one in the wild once, screaming from a rocky bluff above me, but I'd never seen one. I'd always wanted to see one, but now, even though I knew quite well they were shy animals, the thought of an encounter was frightening. It was easy to be levelheaded about such things at home, not so easy living alone in the forest.

The shotgun lay at my side, the shells beside it. Because it was a single-shot, the hammer had to be cocked before the gun would fire. Feeling like a cowardly idiot, I loaded it. I know it was loneliness as much as fear that made me do it.

I tossed the trout bones into the darkness. After placing two thick slabs of bark across the fire, I tried to sleep. I lay on my back, and finally dozed off.

Then I woke up, stomach turning over, heart pounding in my ears. Close behind me something big was moving through the trees. I'd heard it through my sleep, and now I was on my knees, facing that direction with the loaded gun in my hands, hammer cocked. Wide awake, I realized that it must be a deer, probably heading down the steep slope for water, but I stayed there gripping the gun until the animal was well out of hearing range.

There was nothing to be frightened of—I knew that as well as I knew my name—yet half an hour passed before I felt relaxed enough to lie back down and try to sleep. With three more bark slabs crisscrossed on the fire's coals, I stretched out on my side to warm my back. Far away, on another mountain, coyotes howled. Finally I dozed off again, but I don't think I slept for more than twenty minutes at a stretch through the rest of the night.

When early sunlight hit me, I got up. The rocky ground had left my body stiff and sore in many places, and to walk it off I spent half an hour exploring the clearing and eating dry, sour elderberries for breakfast.

I picked up my shotgun and started around the clearing again. First, I circled it—the theory being that when wild birds hear sounds coming from all directions, they're apt to sit tightly in their cover—and then I began to walk slowly uphill through the elderberries, stopping every ten or fifteen feet. Another theory holds that pausing that way flushes birds from cover, possibly because they fear a predator is about to pounce. My quarry here would definitely be blue grouse—big, relatively slow birds, widely known as fool hens—and indeed a half dozen of them burst into flight before I was halfway up the clearing. The last grouse to flush was the simple straightaway shot I'd been waiting for—I wanted to use only one of my shells—and I killed the cock bird cleanly.

Back at the fire, I field-dressed the grouse and tossed the insides down the hill. Then I skinned and roasted it. The breast meat was tender and delicious. I saved the legs, which I knew would be relatively tough and stringy, difficult to chew.

After the meal I used some of the grouse's flank feathers to fashion a lure. By tying a hook to my line, I was able to tighten the turle-knot loop around the ends of the inch-long feathers so they lay back against the shank of the hook, forming what amounted to a small, crude streamer fly.

Down at the creek that afternoon, another skein of geese passed overhead, and I enjoyed watching the water ouzels. I hooked and released at least two dozen trout and kept three, each from a different pool, for my evening meal.

That first full day set the pattern for those that followed: a morning forage for firewood, food, and water, then periods of exploration and sleep. Each day when my chores were completed, I hiked through the mountains and saw a lot of wild country and animals: deer, a civet cat, a badger, a black bear. Birds—hawks, ospreys, crows, ravens, gray jays, a golden eagle, another small flock of band-tailed pigeons, blue and ruffed grouse, and mountain quail—were my favorite company. I enjoyed talking to many of them.

The weather held steady through the week. Nighttime temperatures dropped into the low forties; and from the third night on, after my irrational fears had subsided and I began to sleep reasonably well, the fire would die and I'd wake in the early mornings stiff and aching from the cold.

Shooting another grouse to take home crossed my mind but I decided against it. Instead, I searched without a gun and flushed three birds because I love hearing their drumming wings when they burst from cover. After that, stiff and sore, tired and dirty, I was very much looking forward to home. Since early childhood I'd known I didn't belong in a city. Now I knew I wasn't suited for long-term wilderness habitation either.

On my way down the mountain, I counted seven water ouzels along the creek and heard the pileated woodpecker drumming again. I stopped long enough to have another go at the big trout in the infamous ice-cold pool, but not with a grouse-feather streamer fly. I used a grasshopper instead, as I'd done in our previous encounter, and this time I hooked and landed the fish: an exceptionally lovely male, firm and bright, back and fins speckled with black, the lateral line the color of a dark red rose. I twisted the barbless hook out of his lip and lowered him back into the pool. The trout went back to his life and I returned to mine.

Remembrance of Turkeys Past

In a letter to his daughter dated January 26, 1784, Founding Father Benjamin Franklin proffered this opinion on America's national symbol: "For my own part I wish the bald eagle had not been chosen as the representative of our country." Because eagles stole food from fish hawks, Franklin saw it as "a bird of bad moral character . . . too lazy to fish for himself." In his view, far preferable to this "rank coward" was the wild turkey, a "bird of courage."

Wild turkeys, like collared doves and ring-necked pheasants, aren't native to Oregon. The first subspecies introduced to the state was the Merriam's turkey, in 1961. Those birds were shipped here from Colorado, Arizona, New Mexico, Montana, and Nebraska, and though they survived, they never flourished. Rio Grande turkeys, native to the Great Plains and southward into Mexico, were introduced in southwestern Oregon in 1975 and subsequently established healthy populations in a variety of habitats throughout the state.

Hilde and I started seeing Rio Grandes in the Ashland area about a decade ago, usually from a distance, on our hikes through the mountains surrounding town and in heavy cover near the lake down the road from home. Five or six years ago, flocks began showing up in downtown Lithia Park and then quickly spread into nearby neighborhoods. Now, every spring, on driveways and sidewalks and people's front yards in and around town, the gobblers can be seen in the full-strut mating display meant to impress and attract hens. Human bystanders enjoy these spectacular presentations, but apparently the hens being targeted prefer private mating performances. In public places, they ignore the fanned-out tails and phosphorescent red, white, and blue heads of the flamboyant males.

The first wild turkey flock to visit our own yard arrived late on a warm summer morning in 2018. Hilde and I heard them clucking and purring before they walked into view between our garage and irrigation tank, two or three or four birds at a time, until twenty-two of them—six mature gobblers, the rest hens and juveniles (the males called jakes and the females jennies)— were grazing on the lush green grass between the deck and the birdbath. The three scrub jays that had been feeding on seeds on the deck railing when the turkeys arrived were now looking down from the high limb of an oak tree.

"They're huge," Hilde whispered. "Are they bigger than geese?"

"Yes," I whispered back. "Those biggest gobblers must weigh twenty pounds, at least."

"So beautiful."

"Yes."

I wondered if they realized we were there. The nearest birds were no more than ten feet away, but they paid no attention to us, feeding leisurely, turning in compact circles, crossing paths, clucking softly.

"Dingbat's coming," Hilde said.

"Where?"

She pointed discreetly and I saw the cat walking slowly along the fence line behind the birdbath, an area where he often had good luck with mice. Suddenly, Dingbat froze in place, right front paw off the ground, like a dog on point. Just then the turkey at the edge of the flock, not far from the fence, loosed an earsplitting gobble. Dingbat jumped and turned in a blur and hit the ground running hard, back toward wherever he'd come from.

"Could a turkey hurt a cat?" Hilde asked.

"I'm pretty sure Dingbat made the right choice."

—

We sat where we were and watched the turkeys.

"I think they're eating bugs now along with grass," I said. "They have to know we're here. I'm curious. I'll walk into the yard just to see what they'll do."

"What if they attack?"

"Why would they?"

"Why wouldn't they?"

"You can go inside if you want."

"They won't come up here."

"Why wouldn't they?"

"I want to see what happens."

I stood and took a few slow steps to where three wooden stairs led down to the yard. The turkeys ignored me.

"Good luck," Hilde said.

When I stepped onto the grass the nearest bird, a mature hen, looked at me from six feet away.

"Don't mind me," I said. "Go on and eat."

She did just that.

I walked slowly back and forth across the yard three times, and the unalarmed turkeys gave me space but otherwise ignored me and continued feeding.

Soon Hilde and I went inside and left them in peace. We decided that if the flock came back, we'd watch from inside.

They appeared at the same time for three straight days and then abandoned us, likely having found a greener pasture.

No more than a week later, walking through a residential neighborhood a few blocks from downtown Lithia Park, Hilde and I were surprised to encounter a turkey gobbler marching toward us near the middle of the street, with eight half-grown jakes and jennies following in a loose group behind him and an adult hen bringing up the rear. Just as the turkeys in our yard had ignored me, these turkeys ignored the traffic. Drivers slowed down and swerved around them and, when forced to, stopped to let them pass.

We stood watching the turkeys go by and then turned to follow them. They stayed near the middle of the street and took their time, and at the next intersection they spread out and milled around as if uncertain as to which route would be best. After a minute or two, cars coming from every direction were stopped and horns were honking. The turkeys remained oblivious. I noticed that in cars carrying two or more people, the occupants sat patiently and looked happy, seemingly glad to see wildlife in town. Lone drivers were at best deadpan, with some faces showing frowns or scowls.

Finally, the gobbler chose what looked to be the road less traveled, a right turn up a long hill that led toward a forest of Douglas-firs.

Whenever I see wild turkeys in southern Oregon, I remember a trip I made to South Dakota four decades ago. The turkeys there were very different.

Two generous brothers named Walt and John, from Dallas, Texas, invited me to hunt Merriam's turkeys with them in the Black Hills over a weekend in May. Walt had telephoned me after reading an article of mine in *National Wildlife* magazine. First he complimented me on the article, and then he asked me for help. He and his brother John were trying to teach themselves to form obsidian arrowheads, but in Texas the volcanic rock was hard to come by. Oregon was known for its obsidian. Could I possibly connect them with someone who could supply it to them?

I could and did.

About a month later, an overjoyed Walt called again. He explained that the obsidian they'd received from my eastern Oregon contact was plentiful, of the highest quality, and reasonably priced. Then he issued the invitation to join them in South Dakota: "If you fly on up to Rapid City we'll reimburse you for the trip. Hell, man, we'll pay for everything. Rooms. Food. We already

Wild turkey.

got a local Black Hills guide lined up. Three weeks from today. You got plenty of time to get your license. Every damn thing's lined up. We'll bring the right guns. I mean, it's not like we're anywhere near the bottom of the totem pole. Economic totem pole's what I mean. Far from it! I guarantee you that!"

"I don't know much about turkey hunting," I said.

"Well what the hell! So what? *We* do! I mean, maybe I shouldn't brag, man, but we're damn near the top of *that* totem pole. Wild turkeys are the smartest, spookiest birds alive, but we know the game. You wanna come on up to the Black Hills?"

"I'm thinking about it."

"Think hell! *Do* it!"

I thanked him and told him I'd do it.

"Good man! Don't forget that license!"

I flew from Medford, Oregon, to Denver, and from there to Rapid City, South Dakota, on a Wednesday evening. Rapid City wasn't far from the Pine Ridge Reservation, and, ever since the American Indian Movement had occupied Wounded Knee, I'd wanted to visit that infamous place, to see it and feel it, and walk around and look.

As far as Walt and John went, I'd been in their home state three times in my life, once as a boy to visit an aunt and uncle who lived in Dallas, once as a young adult bumming around with a friend, and once as a soldier. I thought I knew what kind of men they'd be. The plan was for me to meet them when they arrived at the Rapid City airport on Friday evening, which gave me two days on my own to visit the reservation.

The photographs of Sioux warriors in the Rapid City airport surprised me, but the signs soliciting donations to help protect Mount Rushmore didn't. All four presidents carved into the granite of the mountain—Washington, Jefferson, Lincoln, and Theodore Roosevelt—had colluded in the extermination and subjugation of Indians, and Indians know it. I find Teddy Roosevelt's brazen antagonism particularly galling, as epitomized by his infamous 1886 declaration that "I don't go so far as to say that the only good Indians are the dead Indians, but I believe that nine out of every ten are, and I shouldn't like to inquire too closely into the case of the tenth."

I rented a car and found a nondescript motel, where I opened Peter Matthiessen's *In the Spirit of Crazy Horse* and read myself to an uneasy sleep. Early the next morning, I found a café on a lonely two-lane road leading to Pine Ridge Reservation. During my hitchhiking days, I'd been treated well by many truck drivers, so I was happy to see sixteen-wheelers in the parking lot. But the omelet and hash browns were greasy, the coffee was weak, and, as I paid at the counter up front, two customers behind me began a conversation about the Pine Ridge residents, vile racial epithets included.

But the day had dawned clear and cool, and I had the road mostly to myself. Flights of ducks passed high overhead, black spots traveling northward against a pale blue sky. I saw deer, elk, and buffalo, some of the buffalo cows nursing calves in the early light. Just as I passed a sign that told me I was entering the reservation, a coyote trotted across the road a hundred yards ahead of me. A little farther on, a small herd of pronghorn antelope was grazing up a slope of new spring grass.

Driving through the town of Pine Ridge, I saw what I'd been expecting to see: old cars, rundown shacks, stray dogs, and other signs of economic distress. The despair in this place was palpable.

At Wounded Knee, I parked the car and stood alone in a cool north wind to read the sign describing the massacre. In 1890, four days after Christmas, the US Seventh Cavalry killed or wounded as many as three hundred Lakota men, women, and children camped at Wounded Knee on their way to being relocated at the Sioux reservation in Pine Ridge. Subsequently, twenty Medals of Honor, the US government's highest tribute to members of the American military, would be awarded to soldiers who participated in the slaughter.

I'd been there a while, simultaneously trying to think about it and not think about it, when an old car, sputtering, clanking, and lurching, approached from the north, finally rolling to a slow stop beside my embarrassingly new and shiny rental Chevrolet. Two elderly men got out. They reminded me of the people in the large black-and-white photographs taken in the 1930s that I'd seen on display at the airport, showing Sioux survivors of the Little Big Horn battle. These two men had the same lean and erect bodies, the same dark faces deeply creased from long, hard lives. The difference was that they were twentieth-century hunters wearing tattered camouflage. They waved at me, barely moving their hands. When I waved back, barely moving my own hand, both expressionless faces smiled.

"Hunting?" I asked.

"Turkeys," one of them answered.

"No slow elk?" I asked.

"Slow elk" is what Indians often call white men's cattle, and they both laughed quietly at the old joke.

We talked about hunting, and I told them my circumstances. I explained that I'd never hunted turkeys before but had recently read a lot about it, admired dozens of Merriam's turkey photos, and spent hours practicing with a mouth diaphragm call that my hunting cohorts had mailed me from Texas.

"Not so many birds this year," said one. "Bad nesting last spring. Too much cold and rain."

"But enough birds," said the other with a smile. "We got a good one in the trunk. We like the hunt, not sitting around idle on the reservation. A long time ago Crazy Horse said that. It was in a book. A friend of mine wrote it down and gave it to me. It's still the truth."

They got back in their car and I watched them drive away, heading south.

I hiked and drove around the Wounded Knee area for the better part of two days. It was lonely, rugged, lovely country, where the bones of Crazy Horse are said to be buried. On Friday afternoon, not far from Oglala, I hit some bottomland, thick brush with big old cottonwoods in fresh green leaf. I parked off the road and hiked south along a creek bed, thinking it might be a place for turkeys.

I walked slowly and as quietly as possible, making the yelps with the diaphragm call that I'd learned from my tape. I yelped every hundred yards or so, and hadn't gone a mile when a gobbler answered loudly from probably less than a hundred yards away. Within minutes, by answering with a soft yelp every time he gobbled, I'd called him in to thirty or forty yards. Huge tail fanned, wattles fiery red in slanting sunlight, head white as polished ivory, and long beard clearly visible against his iridescent breast feathers, he strutted back and forth on a small, dusty patch of earth between two of the cottonwood trees. I watched him for a quarter hour, talking to him the whole time, until he finally tired of the game and walked off, slowly and with dignity.

That night, I turned in my rental car at the airport and then nursed a beer in the bar while waiting for Walt and John. Walt had given me a brief description to help me recognize them: "Six-footers. Brown hair. No bald spots yet. Jeans and Texas hats. Hell, they'd cover up the bald spots anyway." They arrived a few minutes ahead of schedule, easily identifiable. We talked while we waited for their luggage. When I told them about calling in the turkey that afternoon, both men looked at me skeptically.

"No shit?" Walt said.

"It ain't supposed to be that easy," John added.

Their luggage arrived, including three shotguns in black leather cases.

Except for buses and the two-and-a-half-ton army trucks from my military days, and not counting airplanes, the SUV they'd reserved was the biggest motor vehicle I'd ever ridden in. Walt drove, and the first thing he did after climbing into the driver's seat was clip a small, unfamiliar device to the visor.

"What's that?" I asked.

"Fuzz buster, man. It smells out cops. Anybody who drives sure as hell ought to own one."

"You guys doing okay with the arrowheads?"

"Yeah we are. But it's sure one hell of a learning curve, I'll say that. But we're making progress."

"Arrowheads aren't easy," I said.

"Neither are turkeys. I still can't believe you called one in."

The rooms they'd rented were sixty miles south, in the town of Hot Springs, and we got there in about forty minutes.

They both kept asking me questions about the turkey on the Oglala bottomland.

"Was he a jake?" Walt asked. "You know what a jake is?"

"He wasn't a jake. He had a good long beard."

"There's the motel," John said. "But we got to eat before we check in."

"No way we can eat that airplane crap," Walt added.

At a small local café a few blocks down the road, we all ordered hamburgers, fries, and beer, and talked some more. They temporarily dropped the Oglala turkey as the main conversational topic. When they asked me if I made my living writing, I lied and said yes. I made about half my living writing, and had no idea what they did, and wasn't certain they'd feel comfortable palling around with a professor.

Walt and John were looking forward to viewing Mount Rushmore, and we talked about that for a while. I asked them if they knew about the Crazy Horse Memorial, and they said they'd heard of it but didn't know much, so I filled them in. Less than twenty miles from Rushmore, a 563-foot-tall and 641-foot-long statue of the Sioux warrior on horseback is being carved out of Thunderhead Mountain. The project—still ongoing—began in 1948, the vision of Crazy Horse's cousin Chief Henry Standing Bear. The Polish-American sculptor Korczak Ziolkowski directed the effort for thirty-six years; and when he died in 1982, his wife, children, and now grandchildren continued the work. Crazy Horse's face—nearly 90 feet tall, compared to the 60-foot-tall Mount Rushmore heads—was completed in 1998; the current focus is on completing Crazy Horse's outstretched arm and the horse's mane. If the project is ever finished, it will be the largest monument on earth, some say the eighth wonder of the world. The Texans were impressed and wanted to see it. I decided I kind of liked the two of them and was glad I'd made the trip.

The café hamburgers were surprisingly delicious, and later I would come to wish they hadn't been so good. Walt and John liked them so much that we ended up eating little else but burgers and fries all weekend.

The Texans explained their turkey hunting plans while we ate. The guide would meet us at nine o'clock the next morning at the motel. Driving the SUV on our hunting expeditions and giving advice would be his only functions. When the time came, each of us would hunt alone. The first order of business on Saturday would be getting a feel for the country, scouting things out, and hopefully spotting some turkeys from a distance. In the afternoon, we'd check out Mount Rushmore and the Crazy Horse Memorial. In the evening, our guide would drop off the three of us at the places he'd deemed most promising for "roosting birds"—that is, locating gobblers from a distance shortly before they flew up into trees to roost for the night. Once each of us had roosted a bird—and Walt assured me that that outcome was "guarangoddamnteed"—we'd be dropped off at the same locations on Sunday morning, long before first light, to set up at about a quarter-mile distance and call the birds off the roosts and into shotgun range.

"You must've done some practicing with that call we sent, right?" John asked me.

"I did."

"Can you make it sound as good as the guy on the tape I sent?"

"Maybe. Close at least."

"You mind if I test you out back at the motel?"

"On the call?"

"Yeah. I mean, the thing is you're so *green*. It just ain't supposed to be that *easy*."

"I don't mind a test."

After I passed the test, he handed me a crow call, which looked exactly like a duck call. "This one's easy," he said. "Blow into it any damn way you want and it sounds just like a crow. If there's a gobbler around, or if you think there is but you don't see him and he doesn't gobble after you yelp, this'll turn him on—or piss him off, maybe's a better way to put it. Anyway, you'll know he's there. Get what I mean?"

"I studied up on it."

"Yeah, well maybe you did. But you're still green as golf course grass."

Walt and John had hamburgers and fries for Saturday breakfast and ordered eight burgers to go. I ate a passable omelet. The guide arrived on time, a sturdy middle-aged man named Oscar who farmed for a living and guided on weekends to pick up some extra tax-free cash. He wore khaki pants and a faded red sweat-shirt with a tiger's head embossed on the front.

The Black Hills of Dakota are fine, wild country with a squal-id history. In 1868, the Fort Laramie Treaty granted the hills to the Sioux people in perpetuity. In July 1874, Lieutenant Colonel George Armstrong Custer, who knew there was gold in the hills, pronounced the land worthless and "infested with Indians." Un-surprisingly, in 1877 the US government took the hills back—a year after the Sioux, with Crazy Horse, annihilated Custer at what Sioux call the Greasy Grass Battle.

The day went as planned. On our morning reconnaissance outing, Walt drove with Oscar giving directions; and with bin-oculars, Oscar spotted at least a dozen turkeys, five of them gob-blers, all at considerable distances. He chose three of the gob-bler-sighting locations as the most likely spots for us to roost birds that evening. On the way to Mount Rushmore we ate cold hamburgers.

More than three million tourists per year visit Rushmore, and the traffic showed it. I wondered how many tourists knew that the mountain was named after "speculator" Charles E. Rush-more, a New York City attorney who worked for a mining com-pany in the Black Hills in 1884, or that the sculptor who initially directed the mountain-carving project, Gutzon Borglum, was involved with the Ku Klux Klan and likely a member.

We found a parking space and joined a crowd on the Grand View Terrace. Walt and John had cameras, as did nearly every-body else. The tourists I overheard expressed nothing but admi-ration for the four granite heads and the men they represented.

At Thunderhead Mountain we stopped the SUV and, from a long way off, looked at the outline of Crazy Horse. The very recognizable head was where the most work had been done to date, and Crazy Horse's arm pointing straight ahead, and his mount beneath him, were easy to imagine.

"All I got to say," said Walt, "is the Polish guy who got this idea's an ambitious son of a bitch."

I roosted my turkey that night in a narrow valley with a creek running between hillsides thick with ponderosa pines. Oscar had seen a good-sized gobbler feeding along the creek bank that morning. As he'd suggested when he dropped me off, I set up about halfway between the road and a small clearing down the hillside where the ground leveled off. Not far beyond there, the flat, endless expanse of land east of the Black Hills—the Great Plains—was visible.

I sat with my back against a pine and my crow call in hand to watch and wait. Darkness would come in less than half an hour. I thought I heard a water ouzel call from the creek, and a few minutes later a ruffed grouse drummed, starting slowly, then building to a long, loud crescendo.

Far across the plains a forked bolt of lightning flashed, and the deep rumble of thunder reached me several seconds later. Another rumbling sound followed the thunder, and the ground seemed to quake beneath me. Downhill a few yards in front of me, an elk charged through the pines and two more followed close behind it, and then there were too many to count, and the whole herd splashed across the creek and disappeared into the trees on the other side.

Just before dark, a pair of nighthawks appeared over the clearing, swooping and swerving for insects. Another forked lightning bolt flashed white in the sky, much closer this time, and after the thunder exploded, a turkey gobbled. When I blew into the crow call, he gobbled again, and I judged him to be somewhere near the clearing. I tried the call again, and again the turkey answered.

Now, the intense storm was coming at me across the plains with ever more lightning and ever louder thunder. In the dark I hurried back up the hill toward the road, but the rain came before I reached it. On the roadside I sheltered behind a pine, back pressed against the tree's rough bark, out of the slanting rain. By the time the SUV appeared, the storm had passed.

Walt was driving now, with Oscar beside him, and I got in back with John. The three of them were eating cold hamburgers. I turned one down. Both Texans had roosted turkeys, and I told them I had too. Everybody was happy enough until a state trooper pulled us over a few miles from Hot Springs and wrote out a speeding ticket. Apparently the fuzz buster had malfunctioned.

The next morning, the ground was still wet but the sky was clear. Before first light the three of us were at our appointed places, miles distant from one another.

Two hours later, together again in the SUV, with the Texans eating hamburgers and Oscar at the wheel, we had similar stories to tell. We'd used our diaphragm calls at dawn and the roosting gobblers had answered. After a pause of two or three minutes we'd called again and the gobblers had answered again, but instead of coming toward us they were moving away. I'd stayed where I was and kept calling at intervals, but never heard another response. The Texans had chased after their birds, but each time they called, the answering gobble came from farther away. John wondered if last night's storm had somehow spooked the turkeys. Walt hypothesized that other hunters out in the woods could have screwed things up.

We hunted through the morning and as much of the afternoon as we could spare, and saw few hunters anywhere. Oscar shuttled us to areas where he knew there were birds, and the three of us worked the country in different directions, walking slowly, calling occasionally, then meeting back at the SUV an hour later. I heard nothing anywhere. The Texans claimed to have raised a few very distant gobbles. No one saw a turkey, not even a jake or a hen.

We were all booked on the same flight to Denver that evening, so we had to quit hunting at four o'clock, which would give us barely time enough to make it back to the motel and then on to the airport. Walt sped the SUV toward Hot Springs while his brother ate a hamburger. Oscar and I abstained. Although the Texans registered no grievances with him, Oscar kept apologizing.

"Somethin's wrong today," he said. "I *know* this country. I know the elk, the deer, I know the damn *prairie* dogs! But turkeys is what I *really* know! You all come back sometime. You come on back, I'll give you boys a rate! I'm sorry. *Damn* sorry! Somethin' was *wrong* out there today!"

Most of the way from Hot Springs to the airport, the Texans apologized to me.

"I sure as hell can't account for it," Walt said. "God*damn!*"

"Had to be that storm," John said. "Everybody knows the weather affects birds. Animals too. *Fish* even. Fish e*spe*cially. Look at how bass start bitin' like crazy right before it rains."

I told them about the elk stampede just before the thunderstorm.

"See?" John said. "There you go. See what I'm sayin'?"

"We know turkeys," Walt said. "An' we've hunted 'em in every goddamn weather there is. Hunted 'em everywhere. Texas, Florida, South Carolina, Virginia, Mexico. Sorry, Mike. Sorry you didn't score like you should've. Hell, we hunt every goddamn where. Tell him, brother."

"Just got back from Africa four, five weeks ago. Was it five? Yes it was, five weeks ago. Anyway, we're damn sorry!"

It went on and on. The Texans were confident men, "successful" by any standard American definition and therefore used to getting what they wanted. They meant well and gave what they saw as their best efforts to treat me well.

I didn't tell them that ever since we'd seen the incomplete

monument at Thunder Mountain I'd been thinking about Crazy Horse, and Pine Ridge, and the Sioux hunters I'd talked with at Wounded Knee. I didn't tell them that I wasn't sure the three of us belonged in the Black Hills hunting turkeys, or that I was glad we'd failed.

Thanksgiving Dinner

Though normally it's the scrub jays that show up first for the provisions I set out each day, on rare occasions two or three red-winged blackbirds are already up on the railing waiting for me when I walk out the back door. Most often, though, the redwings arrive later in the morning—anywhere from eight or ten of them to two or three dozen to fifty or more. Flocks of hundreds of thousands have been reported, and they're likely the most abundant bird in Oregon. The colony we know lives and breeds in the cattails bordering our downhill neighbor's pond.

This morning a small flock—maybe a dozen—flew up the hill at their normal arrival hour, circled an oak tree, descended to a low limb, sang briefly, and then flew across the yard to crowd the railing. But a pair of ferociously squawking scrub jays attacked at once from the Douglas-fir near the birdbath, and the red-wings, offering little resistance, took off and disappeared down the hill.

The ferocity of the scrub jays brought to mind the biggest, toughest tomcat I've ever seen. Butch, bequeathed to us from an elderly lady unable to care for him, closely resembled a miniature cougar with its small head with prominent whiskers, short yellowish-brown fur above and whitish belly, and extraordinarily long and graceful tail with faint rings on its tip. Once or twice a month, a neighborhood dog would wander into our yard. If Butch saw it, the dog didn't stay long. Butch attacked and chased dogs easily three times his size down the driveway and up or down the road; and when he caught one, as he often did, he leapt onto its back and ripped out clumps of fur with his front paws.

Butch had replaced a cat named Frankenstein that had never menaced the birds we fed. But we had a strong hunch that Butch would be different, so we trained him to eat on the front porch, on the opposite side of the house from the deck. When he wasn't eating or sleeping at home, he went hunting for mice and gophers in our wildlife preserve.

So Butch never bothered our birds, but a scrub jay discovered Butch's food dish on the front porch. All scrub jays are bold, and this one was exceptionally so. It was longer by two inches than any scrub jay I'd ever seen, and the contrasts among its white throat, blue crown, and gray back were abnormally well defined. Its black beak looked needle sharp; its beady eyes glittered with malice; its high, shrill call was loud and incessant. Heredity is a powerful force, and I like to think that jay might have been an ancestor of the one that now harasses Dingbat.

The giant jay liked cat food as much as it liked pancakes, and whenever Butch left the front porch with food left in his dish, the scrub jay stole some. For days Butch sprinted back and forth in frustration between the yard, our long driveway, and the dish. Finally, he decided to stay close to his food and protect it for hours at a time.

Then the jay went on the offensive. Perched on a low branch of a fir tree, a few feet above where Butch stood guard, it shrieked tauntingly at him. Sometimes, his orange eyes glowing, Butch hissed back.

Whenever the cat dozed off, as cats often do, the jay would swoop down, peck Butch on the head, then sail back to its perch. This infuriated Butch to such a degree that he'd sprint down the steps and up the tree, whereupon the jay flew down to steal more food.

Butch's plight seemed hopeless, and I thought about trying to end the conflict by moving the food dish to another location. But then Butch solved the problem himself. One sunny morning in mid-June he pretended to be asleep, and when the jay dived down from the tree, he turned and pounced. It happened so fast that there wasn't much to see: a few hisses and squawks and a blue-brown cartoon-like blur from which a couple of feathers flew.

When they separated, the jay flew silently away, apparently uninjured. Butch, looking puzzled, meowed and licked a bloodied paw before curling up to sleep.

So the two of them struck a truce. The relationship, evidently based on common sense and mutual respect, developed after Butch set his ambush trap and the jay escaped it. They established a routine. In the morning, the jay sat on the front porch calling for Butch. When we let Butch out and set his food dish down, he'd ignore it. The two of them would immediately begin chasing after one another, but playfully, as if engaging in a game of tag. After five or ten minutes of this, Butch would curl up near his food with the jay perched on the rung of a trellis barely a yard away. Sometimes Butch stirred himself to take a few morsels of food. Sometimes the jay did. My contribution was to stock Butch's dish with ample rations for both of them. Once, when the jay disappeared for a couple of days, Butch stopped eating. Then, when the jay returned, Butch meowed at it, but never hissed. The bird called back softly.

As a pair of acorn woodpeckers fed on seeds, the day's first turkey vultures, a pair of them, sailed into view out over the valley. Even at a distance their inverted wings make it easy to distinguish them from hawks. Their six-foot wingspans and use of warm-air thermal updrafts enable them to stay aloft effortlessly, hour after hour, rarely flapping their wings. Seen up close, most people think turkey vultures ugly. But when soaring in the air, their effortless grace equals or surpasses any bird's anywhere. I first saw them as a child in western Pennsylvania, and since then I've admired them in locations from southern Oregon to Baja. Whenever I see one, wherever I happen to be, I think back on a former acquaintance named Henry, who had once moved briefly to the Ashland area.

Henry stopped by the house on a clear fall day to invite Hilde and me to Thanksgiving dinner. He and I stood on the front porch and discussed which wines to serve. His tastes tended toward the unconventional, so before he left, I asked him what the main course would be.

"Wild turkey!" he said.

I was skeptical. Henry had grown up in the New York City borough of Queens and now lived alone in a rented cabin deep in the woods, miles from town. Southern Oregon was a new and exciting world to him, one he claimed to love very much. Since his arrival in midsummer, he'd spent much of his free time gathering edible plants and berries and trying to learn to hunt and fish—"becoming a genuine westerner," as he put it, "learning to live off the land."

I'd taken him fishing three or four times on the nearby Rogue River, where, using salmon eggs for bait, he happily landed a few previously stocked trout. Because he was determined to hunt upland birds, I'd also lent him my single-shot 20-gauge, showing him how it worked and teaching him how to avoid killing himself or anybody else with it. Henry believed that his dog, Ahab, would help him find birds, but Ahab was a friendly, untrained mutt, also from Queens. Though I thought it next to hopeless, I pointed out areas not far from Henry's cabin where blue grouse could often be found in the fall; and to help him learn to identify a grouse if he were lucky enough to see one, I bought him an illustrated paperback bird book at a used book store. If he ever did come across a grouse and recognized it before it flushed, I figured his odds of hitting it in flight were no better than a hundred to one.

Wild turkey? I thought. "Really?" I asked.

"Damn right! It's in the freezer!"

"Where'd you get it?"

"Up on top of that hill where you told me grouse hang out

sometimes. But a turkey's way better than any grouse. So that's what I'm serving, the turkey! We'll be like the Pilgrims. It'll be a real holiday meal!"

In those days, I ran between sixty and a hundred miles per week and regarded Thanksgiving Day as my annual marathon of eating. So to get in shape for this Thanksgiving, I skipped breakfast, ran ten miles, and then skipped lunch.

In the evening Henry served us dinner. The roasted turkey was oddly shaped and remarkably small, and when he carved it, the meat looked too dark. But I was as famished as I'd ever been and, as always after a run, my body craved protein, so I took a rash and impolite first bite.

Never in my life had I tasted anything so vile. Unable to swallow, I spit that mouthful onto my plate. Everyone at the table stared at me, Henry with his head tilted to one side, as if bracing an invisible telephone against his ear. No one spoke. I took a long swallow of Riesling, both to cleanse my mouth and buy some time. "I don't think this is a turkey," I finally said. "I'm sorry to say so, but it can't be."

An awkward discussion followed. Henry admitted he had shot the bird off the top of a tall dead Douglas-fir. We consulted the illustrated bird book, and he reluctantly acknowledged that the creature on the platter was a turkey vulture. Of course, his mistake was understandable. A vulture's red head clearly resembles that of a wild turkey, hence the name. Unfortunately, a bird's flavor is largely determined by its diet—in this case dead and often decomposing flesh along with internal organs, feces included—so the foul taste was inevitable.

Despite the way they taste, and the fact that many people think them ugly, I regard turkey vultures as splendid creatures. On summer afternoons Hilde and I love to watch them circle and soar on their inverted wings, using the thermals to experience a wild freedom that no earthbound creature can possibly know. The first arrivals in our valley each year come one or two at a

Turkey vulture.

time in March, or in mid-to-late February during an unusually warm year. They stay until October, when they gather in groups of dozens or hundreds before migrating south, traveling as far as two hundred miles per day, some of them reaching destinations in Mexico and Central and South America.

Hilde and I have seen them up close in Baja and wondered whether at least a few of them might be birds that traveled from Oregon. Driving the lonely Baja highway one late November, headed for Loreto, we rounded a bend in the road and a cloud of turkey vultures— hundreds of them—lifted off of the carcass of a road-killed steer. I stopped the Bronco in time to hear the big birds hissing in surprise, or anger, as they took flight. Nothing much beyond hide and bones was left of the steer.

A few days later, on an early morning walk along a beach north of Loreto, we passed a school of a dozen or more bonito, ten-pound fish, dead on the sand. They hadn't been there long, likely having been driven ashore by predators—seals or sharks—during the night. On our return an hour later, turkey vultures were at work, filling their ecological niche to rare perfection. We frightened them off again; and, again, the bonitos had been reduced to skin and bones.

Henry's Thanksgiving meal turned out to be vegetarian, and we did our best to make it a happy occasion. Before the year ended, he gave up hunting and fishing and turned to other diverse passions: a macrobiotic diet, landscape painting, acupuncture, taekwondo, weed growing. Eventually, he and Ahab returned to Queens.

My great-grandfather Brant began his formal education at an Indian school, and, judging by an entry in his family autobiography, he was a tough kid:

"At the school I was sent to many young men were larger than the teacher. It seemed to be their delight to stage fights among the younger boys. After school I often turned down a lane to go fishing and at this turn I fought many a battle with the bigger fellow they matched against me. I was small but quick and could stand punishment; but my hair was long in the old way and it seemed my hair was their favorite hold. I asked my father to cut my hair and it took much coaxing to get him to do it. I insisted and it was done. The hair-hold gone, my opponents were much easier handled. Soon I was able to fish undisturbed."

He was a tough old man, too. During the time he was teaching me to shoot a .22 rifle and catch fish in the creek on his Pennsylvania farm, he had to be rushed to the hospital to have his appendix removed. After two days in the hospital, he insisted on going home; and the day after that, when his son Noss, a doctor himself, came to the farm to check on his father, he found Granddad Brant back behind the barn loading sacks of grain onto a wagon.

To my mind, the barn seemed a much more comfortable and interesting place than the house. It was a square solid building built of raw planks and smelling pleasantly of hay, dried out wood, manure, oil, and leather. Everything inside was organized neatly: plows in two corners, rakes and pitchforks against the back wall, harness hung on shiny nails, and hand tools—planes, saws, wrenches, hammers, screwdrivers, drills, wire cutters, pliers—arranged in wooden compartments along the wall between the plows. There were small kegs of nails, nuts, and bolts; and in a dark corner, three axes with taped handles, their heads shiny from use, were driven into a tree stump.

Granddad also kept bourbon in the barn because Grandma Brant didn't want it in the house. He hid the bottle in a nail keg. I know it was bourbon because I never forgot the distinctive smell that blended so nicely with all the other heavy odors. He sipped bourbon when he talked about the Mohawks and our ancestor, Chief Joseph Brant.

I remember the day he took me to the creek before daylight and landed what he told me was the eighth biggest trout of his long life. I held the fly rod while he lifted the fish out of the water with both hands and held it in moonlight long enough for me to get a good look. Then he released it. "He's been in this pool a long time. He'll stay here. He's an old-timer, like me. Maybe you can catch him someday. Right before first light or right after it gets dark are the best times. Here." I took the rod and fished until, with Granddad's help, I landed a small trout. After that, almost home, we watched an early turkey vulture circling overhead. After the big bird passed from view, he took me into the barn and told me a Mohawk turkey vulture legend. I remember it well because I listened carefully and wrote it all down afterward.

"They didn't write things down in the old Mohawk days," he began. "The people passed things on by word of mouth. Generation to generation. Chief Joseph Brant had a son named John, born in Canada in 1794. He's the one I'm named after. When he grew up, John became a chief too. As a teenager he fought in the War of 1812. In 1832 he died of cholera, a bad disease that came from drinking bad water.

"A few generations later my granddad told me about the turkey vultures. Now it's time for me to tell you, so here's what happened, passed on from the people all the way down to you.

In the beginning, not just thousands of years ago, millions, all the birds were naked. They couldn't sing, because their throats weren't developed yet. Finally they learned to sing by listening to rain falling and wind blowing. But they could talk before they learned to sing, and they complained to the Creator. They were tired of being naked, so they wanted something to cover themselves with. The Creator listened and told them they could find coverings for themselves in a certain place far away. The birds voted to see which one of them should go there, and because he was such a strong flier, the turkey vulture got the most votes.

"But the place with coverings was so far away that the turkey vulture had to eat carrion—dead birds and animals—to finish the journey. When he finally arrived, the coverings were there. Because he was the one who made the journey, the turkey vulture had the first choice among all the coverings, but the Creator explained that he could wear each covering only once. So the turkey vulture started off with the most beautiful covering, but it had so many feathers he could barely fly, so he decided against it. He kept going from one covering to another and found something wrong with each one, until he finally got to the last choice. It was plain and ugly, but he had to either take it or stay naked.

"When they're far enough away from people, birds still get together to talk. Sometimes a bird will tell a turkey vulture how ugly it looks and how dirty its habits are. Whenever that happens the turkey vulture explains that he does valuable work, and that he had the first choice and could have had any covering he wanted—and ended up with the one that suited him best."

Tomato Juice

Feathers are superior to fur.

—Bibhu Mohapatra (from a 2011 *Huffington Post*
interview with Alex Geana)

Acorn woodpeckers live and nest in colonies often consisting of four or five males and one or two females, with as many as a dozen younger birds from previous generations. Our refuge houses a permanent colony, and we often see two or three woodpeckers and sometimes eight or ten of them together flying back and forth between oak trees, eating acorns off the ground, and sometimes storing them in cavities in trees. They also use the birdbath, usually to drink, occasionally to bathe. This morning, three of them came together to eat some seeds, then to drink from the birdbath, and finally to soak themselves one at a time while the other two watched. When all three were thoroughly doused, they flew to the nearest oak and disappeared into the thick foliage near the top of the tree, calling loudly.

When Canada geese flying overhead began to honk, the woodpeckers stopped calling. Seven geese in a tight V sailed directly over our house, then angled downhill toward the pond. The geese circled the pond twice before landing and didn't quiet down until they touched the water.

One of the passing geese had lost a flank feather while passing over, and it fluttered down just beyond the deck railing. I retrieved it to add to my collection of feathers found on our property. Many birds besides those that feed on our seeds are represented: Canada geese, mallard ducks, pheasants, quail, ospreys, red-tailed hawks, goshawks, and golden and bald eagles. For more than a half century now I've been using collected feathers to tie flies.

I first learned about tying flies with found feathers, and fur, from Granddad Brant. That is why, almost a century later, I also use flies fashioned from scavenged feathers when I take his great-great-great grandson fishing.

In the nineteenth century, Leo Tolstoy wrote in a letter to his wife that "the purest joy of all is the joy of nature." Toward the middle of the twentieth century, when I was seven or eight years old, Granddad Brant taught me to fish for trout on the creek that ran through his property in western Pennsylvania. I vividly remember the day I landed my first brook trout on a fly. Afterward, we walked under a clear sky through springtime woods back toward the farmhouse, and Granddad, his arm around my bony shoulders, told me this: "Out here, under the sky, in the woods and along the rivers and creeks, is one place where you can always find some real happiness." Since that day, I've learned, over and over again, in many places and in many ways, that Tolstoy and Granddad Brant were right.

My grandson Jake's angling life began ten years ago when, using a hunk of salami for bait, he tried and failed to catch a perch that had somehow ended up in our irrigation tank. Not long after that, Hilde took him to a lake, where he caught a planted cutthroat trout on salmon eggs. Later that same year, casting a quail feather fly, he landed and released a dozen fat rainbows in a friend's pond near the North Umpqua River. The following morning I drove us down to the river, and, after half an hour of fishing the same fly, he hooked and landed his first wild trout at the Fairview Pool.

Our most recent outing was on the upper Rogue River, water I know well. In chest waders and studded boots, we made our way across a shallow riffle and around a car-sized boulder, and finally crossed the narrow bedrock channel that made the chest waders necessary. Jake, now standing six feet five, found it easier going than I did.

He carried the fly rod, and I carried some truths I didn't want to share: the knowledge that anadromous fish runs have long been in steep decline for a multitude of exhaustively documented reasons; that the dams and hatcheries supposedly built to alleviate the problems have only made things worse; that before Jake was born, there were times when I landed six or eight steelhead a day and now I'm satisfied to hook that many in a year; that back when stoneflies hatched in the water we were fishing today, thirty or forty trout made an average morning.

We stationed ourselves on a waist-deep gravel bar near midstream. A deep, slow channel ran along the opposite bank. Boulders strewn along its bottom created eddies and crosscurrents where trout could be expected to feed. A few yards below our stand, the widening channel became a gravel-bottomed steelhead riffle.

Jake covered the trout water with a small fly I'd fashioned out of mallard and dove feathers. Casting upstream and across, dropping the barbless fly in likely places, he mended the floating line efficiently, and in half an hour raised three small trout. Two turned away before they touched the fly. The third took it, but the hook didn't connect.

To cover the downstream riffle, we tied on an unconventional steelhead pattern, a No. 6 Skunk made of scrub jay, dove, and, for the black body, acorn woodpecker feathers. Jake quartered his casts across and down, then mended upstream after the fly landed and sank, and the improvised Skunk swung slowly through the holding water. He stripped off a yard of line between casts and, when he had reached his comfortable limit, took a long step downstream between casts. I wished hard for luck, wanting him to feel for the first time in his young life the elemental surge of a wild, powerful steelhead on a downstream run.

But I wasn't surprised when that didn't happen.

While Jake fished, a small flock of common mergansers flew upstream so close over the water we could hear their wing beats. After the ducks, a whistling osprey circled high overhead for several minutes. A pair of Canada geese, trailed by six downy goslings, drifted by and stopped across from us to rest behind a curtain of alder leaves that brushed the cold, clear water. All the while, somewhere behind us, a water ouzel sang.

After two hours, we waded out without having landed any trout but nonetheless restored by our time on the river. The water ouzel's song, rippling in the air behind us as we left, called to mind a helpful notion of Thoreau's: many men go fishing all their lives without ever realizing that it isn't fish they're after.

As so often happens, birds had saved the day.

Hilde and I were watching three scrub jays squabble over leftover pancake pieces when a skunk walked out of our preserve and slowly, confidently, crossed the yard, apparently oblivious to everything happening around it. And why shouldn't skunks be self-assured? They're attractive animals that possess a rare defense mechanism enabling them to ward off predators up to and including bears. Recalling the feathery Skunk fly that Jake had used on the Rogue River, I watched the little animal until it disappeared behind the irrigation tank.

Then I also remembered the day I'd added my personal granule of corroboration to the adage that everybody makes mistakes. Driving home from a fishing trip on a cool morning one early spring, I spotted a dead skunk alongside a two-lane country road. Though apparently a roadkill, it looked to be in perfect shape, its winter coat thick and lustrous. The long, coarse hair from a skunk's tail is said to be superior to buck tail or white feathers for tying steelhead or streamer flies, so I coasted to a stop and backed up for a closer look—and smell.

I'd considered salvaging skunk tails before, but every roadkill I'd ever inspected was either too messy or odorful, often both.

When I climbed out of the car this time, I didn't detect an aroma. The skunk lay on its side, facing away from me, looking more asleep than dead.

Taking no chances, I employed a stratagem I remembered reading about in Hemingway's *Green Hills of Africa*. The macho author/big-game hunter had tossed pebbles at a downed lion he'd shot, to be certain that it was dead. I collected my pebbles from the shoulder of the road and, from a safe distance, tossed them at the skunk. Four of them hit and bounced away, and it showed no sign of life.

As I stepped closer, pocketknife in hand, there was indeed an odor—not overpowering, but definitely unpleasant. So I worked as quickly as I could, gripping the end of the skunk's tail in my left hand and using the knife in my right to saw through the tail's base. But the knife wasn't as sharp as it should have been, so the work went slowly; and slowly, steadily, the odor intensified. By the time I was about halfway through, I had to hold my breath as I sawed, then sprint about twenty yards down the road to inhale a deep breath of fresh air before returning to my work.

After about five minutes of this, my perseverance was wearing thin, but so was the base of the tail, and, almost out of breath again, I decided that a quick, hard yank would likely sever the tail from the body. Holding the skunk's rear legs down with the toe of my left boot, I gripped the tip of its tail and yanked upward hard.

But the tail didn't come off. Instead, a spray of greenish-yellow liquid shot at me, and the odor that came with the spray was the most powerful natural force I've ever encountered. I've been tackled hard by huge linemen on the football field, wiped out by enormous waves in Hawaii, and attacked and knocked unconscious by a gang on a city street. These experiences were pleasurable compared to this assault of stench from the skunk.

I stumbled back, temporarily disoriented, gasping for breath. Somehow I ended up behind my car, hands braced against my knees, shaking my head to clear it. After thirty or forty seconds I could see again, but the car itself was nothing but a brown blur. I had the presence of mind to rip my jacket off and toss it away, but that didn't help much.

After a couple of minutes, my eyes cleared and my breathing was back to normal, though inhaling was no longer an involuntary act. I'd dropped my knife but I didn't care. I didn't even look toward the dead skunk as I abandoned my tail-retrieving effort, climbed into the car, and drove away.

Home was about a hundred miles down the road, and I knew I'd never make it unless I did something to reduce the stench. As it had when I'd been sawing at the tail, the odor inside the car grew steadily stronger—from sickening to nauseating. If you haven't experienced this smell even from a distance, it is indescribable, as foul as anything imaginable and then some.

I had all the windows down and even tried driving with my head outside the car, but that was both tiring and dangerous, and it afforded little relief. A couple of years earlier, my bird dog Otto had been sprayed by a skunk, and I'd soaked him in tomato juice, the standard treatment. That hadn't entirely eliminated the odor, but it helped considerably. I saw no reason why the same prescription shouldn't work on humans, so I stopped at the first grocery store I came to, a small mom-and-pop establishment with a gas pump out front.

I parked at the pump, and when an elderly gentleman in faded overalls and a long white apron came out the front door he sniffed curiously, though he was a good twenty feet away from my car. Fifteen feet away, he made a face and stopped.

"Skunk," I called out.

"Just one?" he said.

"Could you bring me out six large cans of tomato juice? I'll help myself to some gas while you get them."

"You think six'll do it?"

"Six, and a can opener too, please."

"I doubt they'll help much, son."

"That's okay. I want to try it."

He backed off a step. "Good idea."

It took a few minutes to complete the transaction. The proprietor left the juice and an opener in a paper sack by the road, and I left his money there, including a generous tip.

A few miles farther along I came to a Forest Service campground, which at that time of year was deserted. Out of sight from the road, I undressed, kicked my clothes into a pile, opened all six cans of tomato juice—twelve quarts—and bathed myself thoroughly, slowly emptying each can over my head, then rubbing the juice in as it ran down over my body. It was cool and rather thick, and while its sweetish smell didn't eliminate the foul odor, it at least mixed with it to create something slightly less repulsive.

I wanted to give the juice a chance to do all it could, so I let it dry, hopping up and down to stay warm. After a few minutes, when the juice had congealed into an uncomfortably sticky coating, I dressed and returned to the car.

It was a long drive home. I hit the freeway half an hour after my juice bath. By then the sun was down and the night air was so cool that I had to roll the windows up and use the heater. This made the smell unbearable, however, so I stopped at a deserted rest area, took everything off but my undershorts, and dropped my jeans, shirt, and hiking boots into a garbage can. It seemed to me that the boots smelled the worst of all.

To add insult to injury, my right rear tire went flat about twenty minutes from home, and I coasted to the shoulder of the road. After a few seconds of panic, I realized that I could wear my chest waders to change the tire.

A few vehicles slowed as they passed by. One large, brightly painted van carrying teenagers nearly came to a stop beside me. "Far out!" one of them yelled. "Weirdo!" screamed another.

I changed the tire and finally made it home.

Protected Acres

> One swallow does not make a summer, but one skein of
> geese, cleaving the murk of a March thaw, is the spring.
> —Aldo Leopold, *A Sand County Almanac*

While three acorn woodpeckers fed on the seeds on our deck, gray wisps of wildfire smoke appeared against Soda Mountain, directly east of us where the Klamath, Siskiyou, and Cascade ranges converge near the Oregon–California border to create an irreplaceable combination of coexisting ecosystems. In 2000, to protect approximately 52,000 acres of the area, President Bill Clinton established the Cascade–Siskiyou National Monument. In January 2017, President Barack Obama added another 48,000 acres to the monument. And President Donald Trump's threats later that year to downsize the monument came to naught. Fortunately, he ran out of time.

Hilde and I gained firsthand knowledge about wildfires years ago, during a backpacking trip in northern California. On our third morning, we were fly-fishing a creek miles from camp when we noticed a cloud of smoke drifting upstream. More smoke, thick smoke, soon followed, and then hot wind, and then we saw the first orange flames. We had no choice but to run for our lives, trees exploding in bursts of flame not far behind us. After two long hours we made it safely out of the forest, our white t-shirts splotched with red fire retardant dropped from low-flying DC4 airtankers.

Today, we weren't in any immediate personal danger as we sat reminiscing about our California wildfire experience and watching the volume of Soda Mountain smoke gradually increase. We also talked about the summer when eighty-one California wildfires collectively burned nearly one-and-a-half million acres in a week and eight western states suffered from dense, smoky air that turned the morning sun red; and about the November 2018 Camp Fire in California south of Redding, which had destroyed almost nineteen thousand structures and killed eighty-five people; and about the contrasting problem faced by friends in Houston, where, while the west burned, more rain had fallen in two days than Ashland gets in two years. These kinds of disasters, we're learning, are quickly becoming the new normal; no matter where we live, we can't escape climate change by running away.

As today's Soda Mountain smoke became a grim, gray-brown haze, we were rescued from a state of mind bordering on true depression by two sets of avian visitors.

A flock of eight western bluebirds arrived in our yard and perched on the low limb of an oak. They studied us briefly, decided we were all right, and fluttered down to the birdbath to splash vigorously en masse for several minutes. No sooner had they flown off again when two perfectly formed and overlapping Vs of stridently honking Canada geese, a hundred birds or more, passed directly over our heads.

We watched them out of sight.

Geese Are More Important Than Golf

This happened years before the trip to Grizzly Peak when I killed my last grouse.

Shortly after dawn one December morning, the clouded sky a pale gray and the winds whistling in icy blasts out of the north, I lay flat on my stomach inching forward over a surface of frozen mud, pushing as best I could with the toes of my boots, pulling as best I could with my elbows, gun cradled carefully in my arms. I felt like a soldier lucky enough not to have a war.

My objective was nearly a quarter mile away, and, with luck, in twenty minutes or so I'd be there. By then my hands, feet, elbows, knees, stomach, and face would be frozen numb, but I could deal with that when the time came. I badly wanted a goose—and this, I thought, was almost surely going to be my day.

I'd scouted Canada geese at this remote southern Oregon lake for two weeks. Through each day, they stayed rafted up near the middle of the lake, so far from shore that to the naked eye they appeared as nothing more than a dark line against the muddied, choppy water. The only thing that would induce them to fly was the approach of a boat; and several times I'd watched hunters roar out from shore at top speed, motors howling, trailing white wakes and thin clouds of blue exhaust. But this strategy not only was illegal, it was also futile. Before the hunters got anywhere near shotgun range, the birds were off the water. I could hear their honking even above the roar of the motors.

Whenever the geese were forced off the water in this way, they circled the lake for twenty minutes or more at an altitude of at least five hundred feet, and then either returned to the lake—

Canada goose.

provided the shoreline and water were both clear—or, if they saw or sensed danger, veered away to find temporary refuge at another lake, smaller and higher in the mountains, a few miles to the north. Nights, the geese always slept elsewhere.

After my two weeks of scouting, I knew that my best hope was to stalk these birds on the flats adjacent to the lake, which was the only way I cared to hunt them anyway. Only their morning feeding went according to inviolate schedule. No matter what the weather or where they had spent the night, half an hour after sunrise the geese appeared out of the eastern sky, circled the pine-bordered lakeside stubble field for about ten minutes and, their wings set and long necks stretched into the wind, settled in for breakfast.

I wanted to bag one—and, because of my respect for these birds, only one—goose this year. Through October and most of November, I'd unsuccessfully hunted one for Thanksgiving dinner. That holiday now past, my goal had become Christmas, barely a week away. If I didn't succeed in time for that, there would also be New Year's Day, just before the season closed. Then, as they say, there would always be next year. This was my fourth year of trying.

The geese were out there on the field now, honking and eating. Concealed by a large rotting log at the forest edge, I'd watched them circle and come in to feed. I was dressed in various shades of brown to match the foot-high grass and stubble, and I'd used my knife to break through the frozen surface to smear my face with mud. While slathering it on, I'd noticed the mud's unpleasant smell. Only then did I remember that cattle grazed this area during the summer.

I'd chosen my angle of approach carefully after walking all the way around the field several times and across it from every possible angle. I'd first considered the problem from a hunter's viewpoint and then tried hard to regard the area as a hungry and instinctively wary goose would. That's not easy, because based on my own observations and experience, Canada geese in wild country are at least 50 percent more intelligent than the average hunter.

Between me and the nearest birds were eight small hillocks—symmetrical mounds about three feet high and ten in diameter. How and why these mounds were formed I had no idea. The first of them lay about twenty yards from the rotting log, and now I'd made it that far. The remaining seven hillocks were spaced irregularly and in such a pattern that I could stay concealed until I was within about fifty yards of the geese's normal feeding area. Twenty-five to thirty yards is ideal shotgun range, and I felt certain that with surprise on my side, I could get within forty yards before the geese began to react. They could get going in a hurry, but they weren't that fast—nothing was that fast starting off—and I'd be where I had to be before they were twenty feet off the ground.

I hadn't done any belly crawling since my army days, and I was surprised by how fatiguing it was. The strain of moving this way results more from its unfamiliarity than from the physical effort involved. As I slithered around the first hillock toward the second, my shoulders and thigh muscles were already tiring. My knees hurt too, simply from being dragged across cold, hard earth. I was wearing ski gloves to keep my fingers nimble enough to work the gun when I made my move, but my hands felt numb despite them. The mud on my face had dried and hardened like plaster, and with that its unpleasant odor had thankfully diminished.

At the very moment I had reached the second hillock and settled in for a minute's relaxation, the frozen surface beneath me gave way and I found myself belly down in cold, wet mud. The hillock was blocking the cold wind, thereby considerably reducing the ground-chill factor, so my protected spot hadn't frozen solidly enough to support 175 pounds of irrational man.

When I rolled over to try to escape the mess, all I did was break through the surface again—on my back this time—and coat that side with more icy mud.

One more roll and I was free, once again on solid ground on my stomach. Holding my breath, I listened. The geese were still out there, apparently undisturbed. Although their muted honking sounded no closer than it had before, I couldn't risk raising my head to look.

About twenty minutes later I was behind the last hillock. My nose was running and my head ached. The mud that had caked me from head to foot had hardened into something like a body cast, and I'd seldom been so cold in my life, not even after slipping off a ledge and falling into a steelhead river in February with the water temperature at thirty-three degrees.

But I'd made it without spooking the geese. I could still hear their contented honking as they fed, though it still seemed no louder than it had from the edge of the woods. I wondered if the numbing cold had affected my hearing.

Stiff muscles straining with the sudden movement, I pushed to my feet and charged over the hillock, simultaneously running hard down the other side, pressing off the safety, and raising the 12-gauge. And what I saw then was at least two hundred geese, well scattered in groups on the grassy field, every one of them looking back at me, and the nearest one more than a hundred yards away.

I realized they'd been aware of my presence all along. And as I'd been crawling slowly toward them, suffering every foot of the way, they'd been grazing steadily off in the same direction, maintaining a safe distance between us.

As they took off, I kept running. Even with frozen feet and legs I had decent speed, but I never got within sixty yards of any of them, too far to even consider wasting a shell. I slowed to a jog, then to a walk, and finally stood and watched the geese climb and form their Vs and circle, honking down at me all the while. As always, it was something lovely to see.

An hour later I was home, soaking in a hot bath.

When I was a boy, my Granddad Baughman shot pheasants and rabbits in the hills of western Pennsylvania with his double-barreled, two-triggered, 12-gauge Ithaca shotgun. What he genuinely loved, though, was his yearly expedition in pursuit of Canada geese. Every winter, he and his friends spent a week hunting geese somewhere on the Atlantic coast, and for several months after returning from those trips, my grandfather talked of little else. I knew they were the highlights of his life.

When Granddad Baughman died, my father took the shotgun; but he never used it, and it finally ended up with me. By then I'd moved to the Bay Area, where the gun was of no use, but four years later when I found out I'd be relocating to Oregon, I remembered my grandfather, Canada geese, and that old Ithaca wrapped in an army blanket in a storage closet.

A few months later, in a southern Oregon combination hardware and sporting goods store, an elderly, rumpled, skeletal clerk sold me a box of No. 2 shells. When I asked him about hunting geese he talked at length, coming across as a character actor playing a minor role in a low-budget comedy. I felt sure he was putting me on. "You want to know where to hunt geese?" he asked, a malicious smile on his face. "That's easy. Klamath Marsh. Hyatt Lake. Howard Prairie Lake. Emigrant Lake. *Any* damn lake. Where you hunted them before?"

"Nowhere."

"*Never?*"

"That's right."

"Well, anyway, it ain't so much where you hunt them as it is when and how. Them geese got *brains*. They got *eyes*. And they can *hear*, too. You light a cigarette in a blind, and they'll see the smoke from half a mile away on a foggy morning—if they ain't already turned around and gone the other way when they heard you strike the match! Oh, you'll see honkers, thousands of 'em, but before you see *them*, they'll see *you*. Opening day's your best bet, before they get their yearly education. Otherwise, you hide someplace you know they fly, you hide there in a good blind with some decoys out, and you wait, and maybe you get lucky. Sometimes they fly a mile high and go five hundred miles in a day. Sometimes they sit out there on the water, and they don't go nowhere far away for two months, except of course for the a.m. and p.m. feed. But I'll tell you this much, son. If you're no sky buster, and you only use those shells for geese, that box right there ought to last you a while."

By the end of my first waterfowl hunting season, I suspected that the old clerk had been telling me something approaching the truth. I'd tried hunting on opening day, which was a maniacal zoo, and I'd hidden behind blinds in remote places on cold winter mornings, a nasty bore, and I had nothing to show for it.

All I wanted was one goose, and in four years I saw at least ten thousand of them. My aforementioned failure at the mountain lake was typical of how my hunting went. Of the twenty-five shells the old man had sold me, twenty-three were still in the box. At that rate, they'd last me another forty-six years.

The two shots I *had* made had come on a foggy day toward the end of my third season. Walking back toward the car after yet another unsuccessful stalk, I suddenly heard geese, and not far off. I knelt at once and stayed that way, motionless, holding my gun in my right hand and the collar of Otto the shorthair in my left. Within seconds a flock of forty-some birds was streaming directly overhead, about twenty yards up and barely visible through the fog. I picked out a bird, stood, and fired both barrels at it. Though this was the sort of shot I'd fantasized about, I missed twice. With their relatively slow wingbeats, the speed of geese is deceptive and, standing there as the flock disappeared into fog, I knew I'd been behind my target.

Eight months later, at home on an Indian summer evening in October, I saw the biggest flock of Canada geese I'd ever heard about, at least a thousand birds, possibly fifteen hundred, flying in two huge overlapping Vs, the lines sharp and black against the cloudless sky, and so high you had to be listening hard to hear them.

They were headed southeast, in the direction of Emigrant Lake, down the road from our home, and before they disappeared from view it seemed to me they'd dropped considerably in elevation. I felt almost certain they were going to put in at that lake for the night.

Canada geese are unpredictable in their migrations, and these were probably a month ahead of schedule. With the lake at its lowest level of the year—drained off for irrigation throughout the summer and not yet replenished by the runoff from storms—stalking would be difficult. I'd be out there the next morning anyway.

Hilde, Otto, and I started toward the lake at 6:30 a.m. If the miracle happened—if I hit a goose—chances were better than even that it would come down in the water, and having Otto retrieve it was more appealing than having to go after it myself.

Hilde was excited about the huge flock too. If we did find the geese, and if I did attempt one of my slithering stalks, she would stay a safe distance behind me with Otto so he wouldn't give me away by an involuntary whine or yelp. His only serious flaw as a hunting dog was his nearly uncontrollable excitability around upland birds and waterfowl.

I was ready, but I wasn't taking my chances very seriously, especially after we arrived at the lake and saw that the hunting conditions there were even worse than I'd imagined. The water was so low that if the geese were there, they'd likely either be on the water or feeding a few yards from it, far from any cover I could use.

The morning was cool, clear, and windless. I let Otto run out ahead for the first ten minutes, to dissipate some nervous energy. After Hilde and I had walked about half a mile, I called Otto back to heel. We were coming to a small bay. We approached cautiously and discovered that there were three mallards—two drakes and a hen—only about twenty-five yards away at the water's edge.

"I might as well try for them," I whispered to Hilde.

"Won't you scare the geese?"

"I'll scare them sooner or later anyway. If they're here, we'll get a good look at them."

Things went perfectly. I charged over the bank and a few yards down the other side, stopped, and brought the gun up as the birds took off. With the sun behind them they were easy targets. Both drakes came down and stayed where they landed. The hen, quacking loudly, sailed across the lake, low over the water, as the shots echoed dully off distant hills. Otto made the retrieves, and coming out of the water his coat was as slick as an otter's.

There was no sign of geese, though. Up ahead of us, another small bunch of mallards, a larger flock of blue bills, and about a dozen birds that looked like cinnamon teal had been spooked by the gun shots, and they all flew off in the same direction the mallard hen had taken.

I was so sure that there wouldn't be any geese—or much of anything else, except perhaps a great blue heron or a careless pair of common mergansers—that I let Otto run free. I kept my eyes on him, though, and I saw that when he trotted up to the top of the rise that protected a larger bay, he cocked his ears and crept forward a few steps before freezing on an oddly hesitant, confused point. He was forty or fifty yards ahead of where I stood, and I whistled him back.

More out of habit than anything else, I loaded the Ithaca and then walked up and over the rise without making any attempt at stealth. The bay, about two hundred yards down the other side, was covered with Canada geese.

I was aware that suddenly I was running, and that all those geese, necks stretched upward to full length, were looking back at me and softly honking. A few of the birds closest to shore flapped their wings as if about to fly, stretched their necks in my direction, then looked at one another and settled back down.

I sprinted hard, the gun clutched in my left hand, my heavy boots pounding down the hill. When I was halfway to the bay, now only a hundred yards away, not a single bird had lifted off the water. Most of them were swimming slowly toward the mouth of the bay, and many were honking loudly.

In my excitement I'd failed to notice that there were geese on shore, too. I didn't realize they were there almost until I was running through them, nearly tripping over them. They scattered before me like huge barnyard chickens. Even though I saw them there and could probably have dropped the gun and tackled one, I was too excited to stop. The birds on the water had turned around and were swimming back toward me now.

Finally the geese surrounding me on shore began to fly, and when I stopped about twenty yards from the water, the ones out there took off, too. I stood there amazed in the middle of a rising cloud of hundreds and hundreds of geese. Their honking came from all directions, along with the sound of the powerful beating of wings; and as the nearest birds lifted off I felt a warm rush of pungent air from their wings.

The gun was up, safety off, and I had the presence of mind not to fire into the flock. In front of me and directly overhead, the air was black with geese. I swung the gun to the right and sighted in on a lone bird about thirty-five yards out, at the edge of everything. In the moment I pulled the trigger, two geese appeared behind the one I'd been aiming at; all three of them dropped into the shallow water a few feet from shore.

Almost as the birds hit, Otto was there to retrieve. Hilde was beside me now. And that was when I realized something else: there was no panic in these birds, not even after I had fired a 12-gauge shotgun. All they did was circle above us, a miraculous mass of life, of beating wings and long black necks and smooth gray undersides.

The best way to describe their honking is to say that it was pure. It was absolutely innocent. After three or four minutes the geese began to climb in one long undulating line, flying southeast toward dark mountains outlined against a bright horizon. We heard them for several more minutes and watched them for a long time after their honking had faded away.

I doubt that many hunters have killed three honkers with a single shot, and I was ashamed of having done so even though it had been accidental.

We walked back to the car with the dead geese and the mallards. Hilde carried the gun and I carried the birds.

It was a while before Hilde and I began to talk about the geese. We decided that they must have come south nonstop from some remote Canadian lake. They were truly wild—this was probably the first sighting in my life of truly wild geese—and we speculated that they'd never been hunted before, or at least not for a long time and certainly not that year. Apparently they were headed south for California, as likely as not the Sacramento Valley, and it wasn't pleasant to imagine what was waiting for them there. The best we could hope for was that I had begun to educate them.

We happened to have a camera in the car. For some reason—habit, I suppose, or a desire to establish the reality of the experience—I felt obliged to take a few pictures of the three dead geese. I've never shown the photos to anyone, and I never look at them myself, because they don't represent what I want to remember about that October morning. Many years have passed since then, and those photos, faded now, are stored in my bottom desk drawer underneath the box that still contains twenty-two No. 2 shotgun shells.

Large numbers of Canada geese live in Oregon year-round. Most couples mate for life, and in springtime we see pairs disengage from their flocks to locate nesting sites. On the pastureland down the hill and across the road from our deck, we see pairs fighting with intruding geese over nesting territory. The big birds honk and hiss at one another, and sometimes bite and maul each other with their wings, causing apparent injuries. When such territorial conflicts have been resolved, the females select the nest sites, build the nests, and incubate the eggs, while the males stand guard.

Geese prefer to nest in pastures and fields—and sometimes parks and golf courses—for two reasons: they like to feed on grass; and open expanses enable them to see predators—coyotes, raccoons, skunks, bobcats, foxes, ravens, crows—from a long way off. Once hatched, goslings stay close to their parents while sleeping and feeding and remain with them for at least a year. By mid-summer, two or more families often join up, and by summer's end, with the young birds flying, large flocks have formed.

At least five million Canada geese inhabit North America, with non-migratory populations on a steep rise. A study conducted in Wichita, Kansas, found that over a twenty-year period—1983 to 2003—the winter goose population within city limits increased more than tenfold, from sixteen hundred to over eighteen thousand birds. Canada geese often live for more than twenty years.

A mile west of our home is a golf course, and the lake with the geese is a mile east of us. My golfing acquaintances often complain bitterly about those geese befouling their fairways, just as my environmentalist friends complain that the herbicides and pesticides applied to the golf course are polluting authentic nature.

My own view is that anywhere and under any circumstances, geese are more important than golf.

Flank Feathers Against a Boot

That mountain quail are the largest North American quail is a verifiable fact; that they are the loveliest quail species on this continent is my own subjective view. That true hunters truly love what they hunt is a concept that explains why for more than three decades and during every season of the year, I hunted mountain quail just for the joy of seeing and listening to them. I found their well-concealed nests in spring, and watched them feed and dust and evade other predators—and fail to evade them too.

On an early January morning during a cold but nearly snowless winter, in a high country of ponderosa pines and scattered oaks and buckbrush with occasional leafless willow thickets in the creek beds, I sat well-concealed on a ridge and watched a coyote stalk a quail covey in the draw below.

She was a healthy, full-coated animal and probably lived in the heavily timbered hills high above the draw. From the pines across from me and a little way downhill, she had spotted the covey feeding in a small clearing next to a steep-banked creek.

Whitish belly low to the ground, pointed nose stretched forward, she crept slowly down the slope through dove-gray early light toward several tall clumps of brush a few yards above the covey. Across the creek from the brush, just as she paused in dark shade to stare down toward the quail, a pair of Steller's jays began to scold from high in a pine. The coyote froze in place for a minute or so, until the jays quieted down and the quail resumed their confident feeding, pecking up weed seeds from the cold ground. They were fully mature birds, their black head plumes straight and tall and their chestnut flanks striped with white as clean as mountain snow.

Finally the coyote lunged at them, powerful hind legs pushing hard off solid earth, long front legs stretching and reaching, big paws landing in a skidding and scraping of spraying dust and small stones. The squawking jays flapped to a higher limb in a neighboring tree; and the quail, the sudden drumming of their wings surprisingly loud in the morning stillness, exploded into nearly vertical flight before veering off across the creek and then turning sharply again to fly in a tight grouping straight up the creek bed just over the tops of the willows.

The coyote turned her head to watch them fly and then, after they disappeared, she turned and walked lazily up the creek bank in the same direction.

In another year at the same location, a half-grown quail stepped into view between a mature bird and a rock ledge. It stopped, cocked its head, and seemed about to peck at a small pile of acorns close to the trickle of water sliding down the pebbly creek bed.

The old resident rattlesnake, four feet long, thick-bodied and healthy, struck from the shaded recess underneath the ledge: a gray-green blur, an explosion of downy feathers. The little bird made no sound other than the quick beating of its wings which raised dust and then stopped abruptly. Then the quail lay on its side and clawed at the air, and then the clawing ceased. One of its wings beat weakly as downy feathers settled to earth, and then it was dead.

Near a mountaintop in yet another year, while a covey fed on berry seeds, a male goshawk swooped out of a Douglas-fir. Soaring in wide, intersecting circles in the warmed afternoon air, the hawk must have seen the quail, but he ignored them until two birds from the covey began to dust on a bare patch of earth.

The hawk's neck stiffened when he saw the quail pair emerge from the protection of the berries and begin digging in the dry earth; and he was into his dive, wings beating for speed, as the target came closer. Leveling off, with wings spread and broad tail fanned out to act as both parachute and rudder, he reached out with sharp talons and plucked up one of the quail. As the quail felt itself lifted away, its legs clawed air and its free wing beat so hard that more dust flew from its feathers, and then the goshawk cleared the trees and was gone.

During one wet spring, on several hikes along a favorite trail in the Siskiyous, I was treated to multiple sightings of a pair of mountain quail and finally found their nest at the base of a small Douglas-fir on a steep south-facing slope. Nestled among protruding roots, protected by a thick canopy of branches, their abode was safe and dry.

I checked on the nest twice. The first time, on a clear May morning, I gently lifted the closest fir branch away and the bird on the eggs stared straight at me, its gray wing covering one eye. For a few seconds I stared back, then carefully lowered the branch and quietly walked away. A week later I checked again. This time the nest was empty except for scattered fragments of shells.

I went back to the nest site many times that summer on hikes and runs; and once I heard the covey calling from a nearby patch of poison oak. When I stopped to look for the birds, I saw a young bobcat not far beyond the poison oak, so intent on the quail that it had missed seeing me.

Low to the ground, the cat covered distance fluidly and quickly. The countryside was wet from an early summer storm, and every ten steps or so she lifted a paw and tried to shake it dry. A few yards from the birds, which had fallen silent, she began to inch forward, almost crawling now.

One quail began the rapid, high-pitched alarm call and several more joined in immediately. The bobcat froze, a front paw stretched forward but not quite touching the ground. Then she dug her paws into the wet earth and shifted weight to gather herself, but when she catapulted toward the poison oak, the covey flushed in all directions, an explosion of frightened birds. The quail were safely into the air before the bobcat reached them.

I watched that covey through the summer. Late one September evening, I sat motionless, my back against the rough bark of an ancient fir at the edge of a brushy clearing where the birds often fed.

They arrived shortly before dark, fourteen birds walking in single file down a hillside in the fading light. But they stopped abruptly when the lead bird saw me, and they never came into the clearing. Instead, they fed into a stand of mountain mahogany up the hillside, likely finding insects there.

I returned on five straight evenings, wearing the same clothes, to sit with my back against the same Douglas-fir; and each evening, apparently growing accustomed to me, the covey ventured a little closer. By the last evening, they fed all around me, unconcerned and clucking softly from all sides. Warm wind moved the tops of the tallest firs on the hillside. I'd been there a long time when one quail, a fully grown adult—a male, I was sure, because of the large size—brushed his flank feathers against my boot as he walked past pecking up his seeds.

Slowly, without any indication that he knew I was there, the quail fed on the seeds until he was several yards away. Still in my field of vision, he turned and retraced his steps back toward me. He brushed against my boot a second time, then fed slowly off in the other direction until he was out of sight.

That barely perceptible brushing of a bird's flank feathers against my boot was a direct connection with wildness, and to me, as to so many others, that kind of rare communion matters as much as anything.

To hold onto what I'd experienced for as long as possible, I stayed motionless against the Douglas-fir until dark. The wind died and the air cooled, and soon a white moon rose into the clean sky above the mountains.

Charlene Swankie, aka Swankie Wheels, speaks these words in the 2020 film adaptation of *Nomadland*. They could have been my own that evening in the Siskiyous.

"I'm gonna be seventy-five this year, and I think I've lived a pretty good life. I've seen some really neat things. . . .[C]ome around a bend [in my kayak] . . . and find hundreds and hundreds of swallow nests on the wall of the cliff, and the swallows flyin' all around. And reflecting in the water so it looks like I'm flying with the swallows and they're under me and over me and all around me. And little babies are hatchin' out and egg shells are fallin' out of the nests and landin' on the water and floatin' on the water, these little white shells. It was like, well, it was just so awesome, I felt like I'd done enough, my life was complete. If I died right then, that moment, it'd be perfectly fine."

Why Hunt?

One benefit of hunting, often ignored, is that it can lead people who do it to places they'd otherwise never have discovered. I'm not talking here about the experiences of insecure wannabe Hemingway impersonators who travel to Africa so they can pose for photos with the big-game animals they've shot down. What I mean is the kind of experience I had when I was searching for a nearby but out-of-the-way place to hunt mountain quail, and stumbled upon an abandoned homestead.

Emigrant Lake—the one that's about a mile down the road from our home—isn't an actual lake; it's a reservoir created in 1924 when an earthen dam was built across a sizable creek to store irrigation water. The impoundment meant that a pioneer cemetery established in 1853 had to be relocated to higher ground, and that a road accessing the country east of the reservoir was inundated.

It's been half a century now since I hiked along the eastern rim of the reservoir on a pleasant June day with my birddog Otto, bushwhacking through willow thickets, poison oak, and buckbrush, and watching for rattlesnakes. We eventually came upon a small creek running down a narrow draw between steep hills thickly forested with oak. Otto drank from the creek, then lay flat on his belly in a small pool to cool himself.

"This looks good," I told him. "This could be the place."

After Otto stood and shook himself, we started up the draw. Dense willow thickets and stands of buckbrush grew along the creek banks, and before we'd gone a hundred yards Otto froze on point a few feet from some willows.

I stepped up close behind him. "Go on," I said.

When he charged into the willows, a dozen or more mountain quail flushed with a loud roar, crossed the creek, and disappeared into the oaks and on up the hillside.

"They're here," I said to Otto. "I'm as glad as you are."

Minutes later, hunting out ahead, Otto broke into a run and immediately treed a bobcat. By the time I got there, the cat had run to the end of a slender limb halfway up an oak tree, and its weight had brought the limb down to six feet off the ground. I knew the distance because I got within a yard of the animal. I'd seen a few bobcats from a distance, most of them running at full speed and quickly disappearing, and here was one close enough to touch, all four legs wrapped around an oak limb. This cat was three times the size of Dingbat. Its grey-brown coat was spotted like a leopard's, and the big, black-tufted ears were cocked forward. Staring into the yellow eyes I saw not fear but rather what might have been contempt.

"You're an impressive animal," I said. "I'll bet you were trailing those quail we flushed. Sorry about that."

I backed off, called Otto to heel, and we started up the draw. When we'd gone ten yards and I turned to look, the bobcat was gone. Soon after that Otto flushed another covey of quail. They too swerved and dodged through oak tree limbs and flew uphill.

Half a mile farther up the draw the oaks were replaced by Douglas-firs, and the fir branches were occupied by hundreds— maybe even thousands—of crows. Otto ignored them. I'd never seen anything like it before and haven't seen it again since. The big black birds showed no discernible reaction to a man and a dog walking beneath them. A few of them cawed, and a very few shifted their positions, but none took flight. I've asked about it and read about it and learned that such mobs of crows are called "murders," but there's no clear explanation as to what that means or why they gather that way.

Not far beyond the crows, the narrow draw abruptly widened

Crow.

into a valley, with lush green spring grass covering its floor and, straight ahead and on both sides, mountainsides of Douglas-firs interspersed with clearings. Three red-tailed hawks circled high overhead, and no more than a hundred yards farther on, close to the creek, was a well-weathered two-story dwelling.

"Dwelling" was the word that came to mind because neither "cabin" nor "house" quite fit. I looked the place over closely, with Otto trailing behind. The entire structure, including the roof, was solidly built of thick, rough-hewn boards, probably fir. Tools leaned against the wall near the front door—picks and shovels, a pitchfork and a scythe, also a small pile of worn horseshoes. There was a caved-in outhouse between the dwelling and the creek. Uphill from the outhouse were the strewn fence posts of what might have been a small corral.

Through the open door, I found a single large room furnished with four straight-back wooden chairs, two rocking chairs, a large wooden table with drawers, and a smaller table underneath a long shelf. On the shelf were a few clouded jars of preserves—tomatoes and green beans, I thought they might have been. Inside the woodstove a half-burned fir log lay on a bed of gray ashes. The table's drawers were lined with yellowed, brittle newsprint from the 1920s, and I read what I could without disturbing the paper. There were stories about Calvin Coolidge, Babe Ruth, and Charlie Chaplin.

The stairs to the second floor were sound. In the small bedroom were an unpainted rocking horse and a faded yellow Teddy bear. There was a double bed in the larger room, a torn mattress on rusted springs. Clothes hung from pegs on the wall beside the bed—a faded print dress, two men's shirts, a green bonnet, and two men's hats, felt and straw. Lined up against the wall beside the bed were pairs of larger and smaller leather boots without laces.

I saw nothing to suggest that anyone had disturbed this dwelling since its occupants abandoned it—presumably when the new reservoir cut off their access to the larger world—and exploring these quarters was as instructive as any twentieth-century American history lesson out of a book. I have no idea who the former occupants were or what became of them after leaving this place; but I contemplated the hard lives they'd lived in a lovely valley they'd had all to themselves, with no plumbing, or electricity, or motor vehicles, or public transportation, or supermarkets. Now, living within a few miles of this abandoned home and enjoying all of its one-time occupants' missing amenities, plus internet service, cable TV, and a smart phone, I sometimes wonder whether I should envy them.

When Otto and I hiked back out, the red-tailed hawks had been replaced by turkey vultures, but the crows were still there.

Baja Birds

The range of Anna's hummingbirds extends from Mexico up the west coast to British Columbia. Though we have them in good numbers at home, the only nest we've ever seen was fifteen hundred miles south, in Baja. We were fly-fishing for sierra off a ledge at the foot of a steep cliff south of Loreto when Hilde noticed the tiny bird flying swiftly back and forth over our heads, always landing and taking off from precisely the same spot low on the face of the cliff behind us.

We stopped casting long enough to explore the cliff face and found the nest a convenient five feet up, built into a cup-like depression in a small outcropping of dark gray rock. The nest consisted of unidentifiable vegetation, possibly dried seaweed, and was smaller than a shot glass. Side by side at the bottom were two white eggs the size of beans.

Just as we turned back toward our fishing ledge, the hummingbird sailed over our heads to her nest, and, no more than twenty yards ahead of us, a pod of orcas surfaced in the bay, most likely to feed on the same sierras we were after. There were eight of them, rolling along like gigantic dolphins, smooth black backs and white chests shining in sunlight.

Anyone looking up facts about orcas will learn that an adult weighs about six tons, has a brain five times larger than a human's, and can swim over thirty miles per hour. As for Anna's hummingbirds, an adult weighs about a sixth of an ounce, with a brain the size of a grain of rice. It beats its wings forty to fifty times per second in normal flight and, due to its super-charged metabolism, consumes half its body weight in nectar every day.

We watched the orcas as the hummingbird flew back and forth over our heads.

I remember another Baja bird.

When I was on a combination magazine assignment and fishing trip in Baja one March, I started each day with an early-morning run, setting out before sunrise and beginning with a couple of miles on the beach, watching the eastern sky over Carmen Island brighten to orange. Then, warm and loose, I cut west along a dusty, rutted road toward the Sierra de la Giganta mountains. Soon the road became a trail, with an arroyo running parallel on my right.

I was halfway down a short, steep hill when I saw the road-runner. He was standing about thirty yards ahead of me, along-side the trail between two clumps of sage, looking back over his shoulder. I stopped in my tracks and blinked, then stared. The bird stood motionless, staring back. I half expected him to beep at me, as the cartoon roadrunner of my childhood beeped at the coyote on Saturday morning TV.

About two feet long, he had a bluish crown, a brown-and-white mottled back, a white-tipped tail, long legs, and large feet. And there was something about the gleam in his eye, in the way he looked back with his head cocked slightly to the side. Like the star of so many of those cartoons I'd watched as a boy, this bird had the unmistakable aura—no other term quite fit—of a wiseass.

I was feeling strong and confident. Decades ago, many days were like that. I knew that roadrunners are capable of ground speeds up to twenty miles per hour (a three-minute mile pace), but I doubted they could maintain that speed for very long. I also knew that they seldom fly. This was rough country, but the vege-tation was sparse enough that I'd be able to keep the bird in sight. There was no chance I'd catch up to the roadrunner—nor would I have wanted to, knowing they're capable of killing rattlesnakes—

but maybe I could make him fly. To my mind, forced flight would constitute a harmless indignity for an arrogant bird.

I quickly plotted a strategy. All conditions suggested a hard, sudden sprint. With the morning sun directly behind me, it was downhill all the way to the bird, and I had the element of surprise on my side. It was possible that this fellow had never seen a human being before, and he'd surely never known one to come straight at him first thing in the morning.

I charged down the hill waving my arms wildly. When I was fifteen yards away from the bird, he hadn't moved a feather. Ten yards. His eyes glittered in morning light. I thought I saw the tall body tense. When I was five yards away, he turned his head and was instantaneously gone. At my feet where the bird had stood, a small cloud of fine brown dust was settling. Streaking through the sagebrush and cacti along the trail, already far ahead of me, was a brownish blur. By the time I'd judged the distance between us at thirty yards, the roadrunner had doubled it.

I started after him at a pace I thought I could hold for half a mile if I had to. Within seconds I was conscious of my labored breathing and of my feet pounding against hard, sunbaked earth. When my right foot slammed into a stone I cursed. Stiff-legged, leaning slightly forward, the roadrunner stayed close to the trail, occasionally swerving around a clump of sage or the trunk of a tall saguaro cactus. About half a minute after I'd started in pursuit, I heard him call—a sound like the cooing of a collared dove, but louder and deeper. By then I'd cut the distance between us in half.

Now we were on level ground, and I tried another sprint. When I was twenty yards away, he dashed off, did a quick left turn, crossed the trail, and ran through some flowering cactus plants with sword-like leaves. Off the trail the earth was sandy, making it much more difficult to run. I was sweaty and out of breath, but I'd shortened his lead again. I'd also somehow cut my right arm on something. Varying his speed but never stopping,

Roadrunner.

the roadrunner veered gradually off to the right, which finally became a full circle that brought us back to the point where we'd left the trail.

Concentrating on both the roadrunner out ahead of me and the ground directly in front of my feet made running more difficult, and I was tiring. The roadrunner crossed the trail, then disappeared down into the arroyo. When I jogged up to the edge, I saw him perched on a rounded boulder fifteen feet away. That was when I should have given up: the arroyo was at least ten feet deep, and twice that far across in places, and some of the boulders dotting its floor were the size of cars. There could be rattlesnakes down there, and even without them, it was a place where a runner could take a brutal spill.

I started down anyway, and the bird cooed again, then began hopping from boulder to boulder with little apparent effort, heading toward the mountains a mile or more away. Every time I climbed down, the roadrunner hopped away ahead of me, and when I climbed out of the arroyo, he sat on a rock looking up at me. Finally I got the fall I deserved, including a long, bloody scrape below my left knee.

At that, I'd had enough. My big right toe was bruised and sore from the rock I'd kicked, and my right arm and left leg were bleeding. I was soaked with sweat, coated with dust, and nearly exhausted. The last time I saw the roadrunner, he was perched atop another boulder, eyeing me calmly and certainly none the worse for wear.

"Congratulations," I said loudly enough so that I knew he could hear me. "Good for you."

I realized then that it was Saturday morning. Jogging back to my hotel, I was bloody and well-battered proof that nature can do a fine job of imitating Saturday morning cartoons.

Saving Birds

We hang up the hummingbird feeder during the first extended period of warm weather in March. Some years, the first Anna's will appear within hours of hanging it, and other years we wait for days, even weeks, before we see one. Through springtime they typically use the feeder one at a time, occasionally in pairs. As the days lengthen and the weather warms, more of them come at a time, and they come more frequently. The feeder holds a quart of nectar—boiled water with a cup of sugar in it—and in springtime needs to be refilled every two to three weeks.

The feeding traffic gradually increases through the summer, and by late August it reaches its peak. Two or three birds arrive before sunrise, and by the time we finish breakfast there's often a steady stream of them flying back and forth between the feeder and the nearby cedar tree.

The traffic increase brings conflict. Despite the fact that the feeder has six feeding stations, when two or three birds arrive at once, one of them establishes dominance and drives the others away with the resolve of a kamikaze pilot. This is probably a carryover behavior: when few blossoms are available, hungry hummingbirds understandably don't want to share flowers, so they aggressively protect their feeding opportunities—even at spacious sugar-water feeders.

And even after a dominating bird has consumed its fill of nectar, it keeps on guarding its food source: from a perch on the cedar tree, it zooms back to the feeder at full speed to chase all other approaching birds away. The only circumstance that alters this behavior is the appearance of black-and-orange Bullock's

*Anna's
hummingbird.*

orioles that occasionally supplement their usual diet of insects and berries with nectar. With an oriole stationed on the feeder, all hummingbirds keep their distance.

In September, the hummingbirds finally come to their senses and give peace a chance. By then it's common to see all six feeding stations occupied, and when a bird or two leave, another one or two soon replace them. Somehow, as summer wanes they finally seem to understand that there's enough to go around.

The only problem with their feuding is the occasional collateral injury. Once or twice a year, when hummingbirds chase each other away from the feeder, the one being chased collides with the glass door between our dining room and the deck and knocks itself out.

When these accidents happen, we're prepared.

Hilde hurries inside. Holding the nearly weightless bird in the palm of my hand, I can sometimes feel, just barely—or do I just imagine it?—the rapidly beating heart. I'm happy to know it will survive. From our long experience with such incidents, we've concluded that with the feeder only a few feet from the door, birds being chased from their perch are never traveling fast enough to kill themselves.

Hilde returns with the small straw basket we always use and places it between us on the tabletop. When I lower the bird gently to the bottom of the basket, it either stands there motionless or topples onto its side. We cover the basket, usually with a section of the morning paper. After a few minutes, when we lift the paper off, the tiny bird flies straight up, hesitates briefly, then speeds across the yard to a perch in the cedar tree.

Through the years I've written dozens of articles for outdoor and environmental magazines—*National Wildlife*, *High Country News*, *Gray's Sporting Journal*, among others. In the 1970s and 80s I was happy to serve as a special contributor to *Sports Illustrated*, because it gave me an opportunity to publish pieces in a magazine with millions of readers, many of whom were rarely exposed to the subjects I most wanted to write about: irresponsible logging practices, endangered species, polluted rivers, ethical hunting and fishing, wilderness preservation, gun control. I remember how delighted I was when my editors agreed to let me do a story about a fellow Oregonian named Dave Siddon, whose life was dedicated to rehabilitating sick, injured, and orphan wildlife, primarily birds.

"I'm doing what I want to do," he explained soon after we met. "I figured out a long time ago that doing what you really enjoy is a lot more important than getting rich, so I'm here, and I'm happy."

In 1981, Siddon founded the Wildlife Images Rehabilitation and Education Center located near the small town of Merlin, Oregon, on the Rogue River. The center—still in operation, though now directed by David Siddon Jr. since his father's death in 1996—serves as a clinic, animal sanctuary, and educational outreach facility. By the time I interviewed him in 1982, Siddon had been saving wildlife for forty-two of his fifty-one years and had returned more than four hundred injured birds and animals to the wild, among them three bald eagles and nine golden eagles.

When Hilde and I began our long conversation with him on a drizzly winter day, Siddon was standing on a gravel driveway between his ranch-style house and the center's barn door, a chunk of raw chicken in his hand, looking up at an American kestrel—also known as sparrow hawk—perched atop a twenty-foot pine tree. "This guy never *wanted* to leave us," he said. "We turned him loose five years ago and he's still hanging around. Watch this." He tossed the chicken, and before the meat had reached the apex of its trajectory, the little hawk—which often hunts from trees—swooped down, clutched the meat in its talons, banked steeply, and soared off toward the river, all in less than a second's time.

"Did you see that? Did you see it?" Siddon exclaimed. He was well over six feet tall, ruggedly built, with a thick head of white hair, and when he talked about his birds he always smiled. And he talked a lot about his birds. "It's tough for them at this time of year," he said, looking after the kestrel and grinning broadly. "They can't do a lot of soaring in this weather, and prey species are scarce, so I help out once in a while. Look here in the barn now."

Inside the barn was a blind spotted owl named Ollie, standing on the concrete floor, head turned toward the open door. Siddon walked over, dropped another piece of chicken near him, and whistled softly. At the signal, Ollie grabbed the meat with a talon, then turned and walked away to find a place to enjoy his meal in solitude.

"Ollie's a permanent resident, of course," Siddon explained. "We're able to save about 60 percent of the birds and animals we get; and about 90 percent of the ones that do survive can eventually be released. If we think there's at least a fifty–fifty chance a creature will make it, we release it.

"My feelings are strong on that subject. I don't believe in keeping wild creatures penned up, and I don't believe in captive wildlife breeding either, unless there's simply no other way to preserve a species. What they're doing with the California condor right now would be an example of that. But I know of people who are crossbreeding peregrine falcons with other species, hybridizing them. When the crossbreeds escape from falconers—and some will—what will be the result on native gene pools? They've already gone a long way toward ruining various species of fish with hatcheries. Whether you believe in God or in the scheme of nature, you shouldn't manipulate. Let nature take its course.

"When we do have to keep a bird or animal, though, we make good use of it in our educational programs—but the wilderness is where they belong. And we've treated just about everything here over the years—deer, bears, cougars, raccoons, weasels, bobcats, turtles, skunks, foxes—you name it and it's probably been here. Right now, though, most of our guests and patients are birds."

Those guests and patients had been brought to the center by private individuals who knew of Siddon's work, and by police and federal wildlife officials. Most of the injuries Siddon treated were the result of human activity. Birds of prey in particular suffer at our hands. On slow days, some so-called hunters sometimes act on the temptation to regard soaring hawks and eagles as targets of opportunity. Because several species of hawks and owls hunt near roads, many of them are killed or injured by passing traffic. Birds of prey are also especially susceptible to the poisoned baits and leghold traps set out by ranchers for coyotes. In the first of several wooden pens behind the center's barn were four magnificent bald eagles. "Two of them are gunshot victims," Siddon said, his smile fading for the first time. "That one over there, on the left, injured his wing when he flew into a power line over near Klamath Falls. My theory is that when birds look at wires, they think they're seeing twigs, and they think they can fly right through them. The other bird, back there in the shadows, caught a fish with about fifteen feet of monofilament line in its mouth, and he ended up with the line wrapped around his wing, crippling him."

Farther along were several golden eagles, two of them also gunshot victims. They were looking well and would soon be released to the wild. So would a large, lovely female golden eagle that a woman had found about eighty miles away, in a meadow near a mountain lake. She drove to the center, holding the nearly starved bird on her lap. Apparently it, too, had flown into a power line and broken a wing. Siddon fed the bird back to health and implanted steel screws in the injured wing. It would be ready for release in the spring.

"The eagle over there," Siddon said, pointing to another large female golden eagle that had been screeching continually for several minutes, "is imprinted. That means she grew up with humans and associates with them instead of with her own kind. We'll never be able to release her. But she more than pays her own way. She was featured in a John Denver television special, and not long ago she made a Ford Thunderbird commercial. She's a beautiful bird now, but when we got her, she was suffering from malnutrition. Her owners—she'd been stolen off a nest—had been feeding her bologna, which doesn't contain enough protein for eagles."

Beyond the pens stood a large cage containing various species of hawks, including Happy, who according to Siddon was probably the most widely photographed red-tail on Earth. Tens of millions of Americans saw her in Buick commercials and print ads.

An accomplished independent filmmaker himself, Siddon had contributed segments to both *The American Sportsman* and *Last of the Wild* television series. All proceeds earned by Siddon's birds went to the center. Public donations also helped pay the bills, and the center has always been healthy financially.

"My wife Judy, and twenty-eight-year-old son, David Jr., work with me, and we've hired a young biologist for our educational programs," Siddon told me. "They give their presentations— films, talks, and exposure to the living birds and animals—in school assemblies across the country. We've been in thirty-two states so far, and last year we reached about six hundred thousand youngsters. We have a traveling Birds of Prey program, a Vanishing Species program in Colorado, and a Watchable Wildlife program here in Oregon. We want to add two more Birds of Prey programs and two on Animals Nobody Loves—skunks, vultures, and the like. When you can get to young people and show them a hawk or eagle up close, they're a lot less likely to shoot one if they ever take up hunting. And they're going to be a lot more likely to learn to love wild creatures, not to see them as something to destroy, or exploit, or ignore."

In preparation to open Wildlife Images to the public for guided tours and photography workshops, Siddon was building new pens for his birds that would offer better viewing opportunities.

"In a way, I'm living my father's dream here," he said. "He was born in Tennessee and raised and cared for birds all his life. I grew up in southern California, San Fernando Valley, and our backyard was always full of cages. My father treated injured birds, and he raised doves, finches, and parakeets and sold them to make money for vacations. He worked as a mechanic, but he always hoped to be able to devote all his time to birds. But the Depression came along, and then the war. He knew a lot, and I learned from him. I haven't had any formal training to speak of in what I do here, but I had my first patient when I was nine years old—a mourning dove. Next there was a mockingbird. When I was twelve I remember a barn owl, and by the time I was seventeen I was up to golden eagles. Look! See up there?" He pointed to a screech owl sitting on an oak tree limb, staring down from thirty feet away. "We released her a while back, but she's not sure she wants to leave either."

In another line of pens was an assortment of owls, and a vulture with a bad left leg. Siddon reached into one of the pens and came out with a pygmy owl, which is barely larger than a sparrow but has formidable talons and bright yellow eyes. "Ounce for ounce, he's as deadly as any predator alive," Siddon said. "Around here we have to remember that all of these are wild creatures, not pets. I almost lost an eye to a golden eagle once, and a thumb to a raccoon."

Walking back toward the barn, Siddon related a story that really made him smile. "But, of course, it's their wildness we want to preserve," he began. "Two years ago, a state biologist brought me a bald eagle from up near Glide, along the North Umpqua River. It was one of a pair that had been observed in that area. The bird was almost dead when my friend got him here by pickup on a Sunday morning. He couldn't even hold his head up. It was strychnine poisoning. I could smell it right away. He'd probably been at a tainted carcass set out for coyote bait. We force-fed him for weeks, finally nursed him back to health. When it came time to take the bird back where it came from to release it—this was in April—the press and television people came out to watch.

"That always makes me a little nervous, because I'm afraid a bird might just fly up to the nearest tree limb and sit there looking back at me. But everything went perfectly. Like they said the next day in the Roseburg paper, Walt Disney couldn't have written a better script. When I set the eagle free, he sailed straight across the river. He was full of energy, really going!" At this point, Siddon began to flap his arms like wings, trying to recreate the moment. "He caught a thermal and went up eight hundred or a thousand feet and then circled for a while. Then he caught *another* thermal and rose another thousand feet. Minutes had passed by then. When he finally leveled off up there, he was just a speck. And then another eagle appeared, sailing in from somewhere! Suddenly there were two of them there, and off they went together. Why, by that time the woman running the television camera was in tears. It was perfect all right—better than perfect! That's what it's all about!"

In a nearby pen, a golden eagle flapped its powerful wings. A hawk called shrilly, and Siddon glanced at the pens and then looked up at the sky, remembering the bald eagle. No wonder he was happy.

Footnote: Just recently, some of the patients undergoing treatment at Siddon's clinic were casualties of work being done by our son Pete, an arborist employed by the city of Ashland. Early on a recent summer morning, he and his boss were taking down a dead alder in Lithia Park. When the tree hit the ground, a nest of baby squirrels in a cavity near the treetop was thrown into Ashland Creek. Pete saw the nest in time to wade in after it and save the little animals. He left the nest near the downed tree for the rest of the day, but when the mother failed to appear, Pete's boss drove the squirrels fifty miles up I5 to Wildlife Images. They were soon released back into the wild.

Survival

From poisoned eagles to the occasional hummingbird that collides with glass, there's always something poignant about wild creatures living all or part of their natural lives in the midst of what we call civilization. A mile from our home, barn swallows build nests on the underside of an I5 freeway overpass. Once I watched a squirrel busily storing acorns in a golf cart parked beside an oak tree. Several years ago I saw the sickening sight of dozens of spring Chinook salmon trying to leap over a new dam in their river. Time after time, fish after fish, they bounced off a concrete wall in their futile efforts to continue upstream to spawn.

Many springs ago, I discovered a killdeer nest adjacent to Southern Oregon University's all-weather track. The track enclosed a football field, with a narrow border of pebbles between the grass and the running surface, probably to facilitate drainage when the field was watered. On the fringe of the pebbled border was where the birds had nested.

Killdeers, a member of the plover family, are brown birds with white foreheads, throats, and undersides; two black neckbands; and orange tails. Their name is supposed to sound like their call—two strident screeches, persistent and loud. Usually killdeers are found in pastures, mud flats, or lake borders, but—like geese—they occasionally turn up on golf courses and athletic fields.

The killdeers that chose to hatch their young alongside the track were bound to have trouble. Their nest was nothing more than a slight depression, and the four eggs in it—gray with irregular black spots—matched the pebbles perfectly.

Killdeer.

On an early weekday morning I was running 440s, and each time I rounded the turn into the homestretch, the two birds appeared, turning close circles over my head, screeching furiously. But by the time I'd completed the lap, they'd disappeared. An elderly couple showed up and began jogging. The killdeers circled over them too, and from a distance I saw precisely where they were coming from.

I walked across the field, and even though I knew where to look, it was difficult to spot the eggs. Only their perfect ovoid form distinguished them from the pebbles. I doubted that the eggs had as much as a fifty–fifty chance to hatch in such a location, and for the next two weeks I thought about them often.

Ordinarily, I worked out at the college only once or twice a week because the track was often crowded and running on it was always dull. But now I began going there every day, sometimes even two or three times a day, to check on the nest and its occupants.

I did a lot of running, but my workouts were nothing compared to what the killdeers went through. Each time a runner plodded or sprinted by their nest, they rose to wheel above the intruder in nervous circles, screaming all the while. On some days there was an almost ceaseless stream of runners, so the birds rarely got to spend an uninterrupted minute with their eggs. When I passed their nest myself, I detoured to an outside lane, but that was scant consolation for them.

As far as I could tell, no one else had noticed the eggs. Other runners paid no more attention to the killdeers than they did to the many starlings, blackbirds, and crows in the area. I decided not to point the nest out to anyone, except in a case of impending disaster. All things considered, human ignorance would likely be the killdeers' best defense.

Occasionally, runners had dogs with them, and when one came anywhere near the nest, one of the killdeer parents would feign an injury to distract it. The bird would hop toward the middle of the football field, dragging a limp wing through the grass and screeching in apparent agony; and then, with the dog almost upon it, it would rise in flight. Once, with a pair of dogs on the scene, both birds simultaneously got into the act. Their hoax never failed.

One Sunday morning, a golfer was practicing chip shots on the football field. He was aiming at the long-jump pit, just a few yards from the nest. An errant shot came within inches of landing on the eggs, and a couple of others rolled close by. I was about to tell the golfer of the nest when he finally collected his practice balls and headed home.

Later that afternoon, I returned to the track to check things out again. When I arrived, a young man in a straw hat had just finished cutting the grass on the football field with a tractor mower. I ran over, expecting the worst. As I approached, the killdeer couple fluttered up, screeching as usual, and began darting and swooping in their customary tight circles, quick and graceful on their long, pointed wings. One egg had been crushed by the mower, but three had survived.

Two days later, pieces of shell were scattered over the pebbles and there was no sign of life in the immediate area. Young kill-deers leave the nest almost as soon as they hatch, so I had hopes that all three tractor-mower survivors had made it.

Soon I knew they had. Walking across an adjacent field, I saw the killdeer family—two thin and weary-looking adults, heads bobbing as they marched into a thick clump of weeds, followed by three tiny young ones scrambling along behind them. They disappeared, and I imagined them staying there for a long while to recuperate, enjoying their peace and quiet. By then they must have been at least as tired of the track as I was.

It's always enjoyable, and sometimes enlightening, to watch what happens down the hill at our neighbor's pond. Every so often at first light in midwinter, a coyote or two emerge from brushy cover, trot quickly by the farmhouse, and disappear into cattails or the brush beyond to hunt. Ospreys, having discovered the pond's bass and bluegills, circle over the water for half an hour or longer at a time. They seldom dive for fish, and when they do they rarely succeed, but they keep coming back. Bald eagles make rare appearances, also looking for fish. Egrets, whiter than snow, circle and land with their long necks tucked in and their spindly legs extended behind them. After landing, they station themselves at water's edge, motionless, hoping for a small fish in shallow water, or a frog. From late fall through early winter, dozens of mallards use the pond, hens quacking loudly and all of them busily tipping to feed.

In late winter, Canada geese appear in numbers over our valley and, slowly but surely, the vocal flocks break into smaller groups and eventually into pairs. By late February or early March, a few pairs establish temporary residence at the pond. Once they've built their nests among the cattails, they aggressively drive off any other geese that land on or anywhere near the pond, and they protect their young from the skunks, foxes, raccoons, and great-horned owls that mostly hunt at night.

During daylight hours, we watch the parents rear their off-spring. The goslings grow and develop quickly, able to walk and swim soon after hatching. At first, on both land and water, their parents keep them close. When the family leaves the cattails to feed on grass, or walks from where they've been feeding down to the pond for a swim, one parent leads the way and the other brings up the rear, the goslings marching in single file between them. At this stage, the parent geese attack any bird or animal—or human—that dares come near.

After about ten weeks, the goslings can fly and begin show-ing signs of independence. When they've grown into strong fli-ers, Hilde and I know what's bound to happen next. Early some fall morning, we'll look down at the pond and see that all the geese are gone, and we'll be happy for them.

But one year more than two decades ago, we experienced a unique Canada goose departure day. Back then, two domesticat-ed geese were permanent residents of the farm, big white birds with clipped wings that had to weigh at least twenty pounds each. For comparison, the average Canada goose is little more than half that size.

When the Canada geese had arrived earlier that year to build nests in the cattails and raise their goslings, the farm geese that resided in the pond made no attempts to interfere. As had been the case in previous years, the permanent residents simply ig-nored the interlopers, and the visiting geese returned the favor. The two varieties never intermingled on the water, or in the cat-tails, or while grazing on grass. Hilde and I had long ago conclud-ed that geese were like certain people, the ones who decide that fellow human beings who don't quite look right—which is to say, not exactly like them—can be endured, but only from a distance.

But this year, things worked out a little differently. There were only two pairs of Canada geese, with ten goslings between them, living at the pond. Late one night in early summer, I was awak-ened to a sound I love: howling coyotes. I'd never heard them so close to the valley floor in summertime before. I guessed there were two of them, their howls and infrequent yips answering one another, and I judged them at first to be a mile or two away, in the hills to our north. But as I lay in bed listening, they kept coming closer. When the howling and yipping stopped, the animals couldn't have been more than a quarter mile away.

I'd nearly fallen back asleep when I heard the loud, incessant honking of Canada geese. The commotion lasted only ten or fifteen seconds. I thought I knew what had happened, and at first morning light I was at the dining room window, using binoculars to check out the pond, cattails, and surrounding pastureland.

Near the pond, a few feet apart, were two piles of bloody feathers. About half an hour later, one of our domestic geese emerged from the cattails closely followed by two of the Canada geese babies, with the second domestic goose close behind. Hilde and I watched through the window as we breakfasted. What had happened seemed clear. The coyotes had killed all four adult Canada geese and most of their offspring, but the domestic geese and two wild goslings had somehow survived, and by morning the orphans had been adopted.

For the next three months, the four blended-family members were rarely separated by more than a few feet. They ate grass together, swam together, walked into and out of the cattails together, and the coyotes never came back. In September, the Canada geese siblings began making training flights out toward the lake, at first disappearing for only minutes at a time, but by mid-October extending their flights to an hour or more. They always returned by the same route, side by side, low in the sky, honking as they circled the pond before landing on the water to join their adoptive parents, who had watched them leave and waited patiently for their return. In early November, though, the two young Canada geese left and never came back.

An Old Man's Pond

> Fishermen, hunters, woodchoppers, and others, spending
> their lives in the fields and woods, in a peculiar sense a part
> of Nature themselves, are often in a more favorable mood for
> observing her, in the intervals of their pursuits, than philoso-
> phers or poets even.
>
> —Henry David Thoreau, "Higher Laws"

A hunter I met by chance wasn't the type of old man to appeal
to sentimentalists and was certainly no subject for the Norman
Rockwell *Saturday Evening Post* covers from my boyhood. He
was short, dark-skinned, white-haired, and foul-mouthed. I enjoyed his company only once, on a southern Oregon fall afternoon.

It was hot, and I was walking a rarely used and deeply rutted
logging road into some steep, rough country. Otto the shorthair
was somewhere up ahead chasing a squirrel.

"Ought to keep your damn mutt close!" the harsh voice said
from behind me.

I jumped and turned. Dressed in tattered, baggy denim pants
and a much-too-large green t-shirt, he was about as old as I am
now, and he stood there glowering up at me. Protruding from
the t-shirt sleeves were two lean and muscular brown arms. He
could have been an Indian—Modoc? Klamath?—and, except for
the scowl on his face, he reminded me of my great-grandfather
Brant. The double-barreled 12-gauge that he carried across his
shoulder looked huge, creating the impression of a child packing
a small cannon. His own dog, a black Lab, was closely at heel.

"There's grouse along this road," he said, "if that's what you're looking for."

"I've been in here four or five times and never seen a bird along here yet."

"Bullshit," he said. "I've been in here four or five hundred times."

"Then I guess you should know."

"They're sure as shit here. But I don't hunt roads myself."

I whistled Otto back and scolded him to heel. He was interested in the Lab, a female, but he obeyed.

"Young dog," the old man said. "At least he's trained some."

"I work with him every day."

"I hope so. Come on along with me if you want."

We walked on up the road together, leaning forward to compensate for the steepness, and I think he was showing off by setting an impressive pace. The road curved up the south side of a mile-long canyon. A small creek ran through the canyon, fifty yards or so below us, the steady trickle of water looking like tinfoil when sunlight caught it in the open spaces between clumps of deer brush and pine.

The old man swore at nearly everything, and he did so proficiently, using his obscenities and profanities as verbs, adverbs, adjectives, and nouns. Occasionally he managed to work in a more original, if misused, part of speech. "I love to hunt," he said for no apparent reason and in a tone of voice that implied I'd accused him of being unfaithful to his pastime. "No matter what some goddamn idiots say, I love it. These anti-hunting people, these asshole vegetarians in leather shoes and fur coats. Most hunters these days are assholes too. But they're no worse than those others."

"I like hunting too," I said. "It's my second season, my first with my own dog."

He swore again, more violently. Then, "Don't ever hunt without a dog!"

"I didn't, I had a friend with a dog," I explained.

Behind us now a Jeep was grinding along the logging road. The old man swore quietly. We stood off to the side in the warm shade of a Douglas-fir and watched the vehicle pass, a new model carrying two young men who could easily have been the old man's grandsons. A case of beer was conspicuous between two pump-action shotguns leaning against the rear seat. They waved at us and smiled, that special supercilious smile young people reserve for the aged—the smile I see often enough myself these days.

It surprised me when the old man managed half a smile and waved back.

The Jeep ground ahead and finally rounded a bend, leaving us in its exhaust fumes and dust. This time the old man swore ferociously. "No dog!" he said. "Fat asses and pot bellies! *They* won't get any birds! Drinking goddamn *beer!* A *Jeep!* I *hate* the sound of motors out here!"

I hunted with him through the afternoon. He showed me the best ways to work the cover on the steep slopes, and on the brushy draws near water, and on the high flats where the springs spread out into small marshes and the grass was heavy enough to provide cover for birds. It was hot, hard work. I was sweat soaked, my calves ached, and my hamstring muscles quivered, yet the old man never appeared to tire.

His technique was simple and sensible. We would get on the downhill side of wherever he knew there might be birds and send the dogs up to hunt the cover. Otto learned from the older dog as I learned from the older man. The terrain was steep enough that the grouse always flushed downhill. We'd hear the dogs quartering through the cover, and then the loud drumming of wings, and suddenly a bird would appear, or sometimes two or three—fast grayish blurs that burst out, sailed by, and curved away at difficult angles to disappear behind the nearest trees. We would hear them, suddenly see them, get the guns up, swing and shoot, and the birds were either hit and down or out of sight.

In two hours, after ten shots, I had one cock blue grouse. The old man had used three shells to kill a cock ruffed grouse and a hen blue. He handled his oversized gun with speed and ease.

"I pass up the easy shots," he explained at the end. "Anybody should hit the easy birds."

We had worked our way around to the southwest side of the mountain. About five hundred feet below the gray rock peak, we sat in the shade on a fallen log by a pool of spring water. It was icy water, clean and delicious. The old man had laid the dead birds out on the log between us. The dogs lay stretched out in a puddle cooling their bellies, staring at us with their brown, intensely interested birddog eyes. Tired or not, they wanted to hunt.

"I love dogs," the old man commented.

"I guess I forgot my knife," I confessed.

He swore gently. "I'll do it," he said.

He field-dressed the three grouse, using his pocketknife to cut slits below the breastbones. All three birds were stuffed with berries and seeds.

He placed them back on the log. Grouse might be the only creatures as beautiful dead as they are alive; or it might be that we seldom get close enough to living wild birds to really see them. But we looked closely at these three now, lined up on the brown bark. The cock blue was actually a grayish color mottled with blue, white at the shoulders, a bright orange patch of skin above its glassy eyes. The smaller hen blue was mottled brown. Both birds had a black tail with the broad gray band at the tip. The ruffed grouse, reddish above, yellow-brown below, barred tail fanned out, was the loveliest of all.

"That's plenty for today," the old man said. "Let's head back."

On the way back out around the mountain to the Forest Service road where I'd parked, he showed me a pond I'd never known was there. An optimist might have called it a small lake. Water from dozens of springs that drained down the mountain's western slope converged and met, then spread out again to shallowly cover a four-or-five-acre flat closely surrounded by thick timber. The old man said that sometimes there were mallards on the water, dozens or even hundreds of them, and it wasn't unusual to see Canada geese. "It's the season," he said. "But no hunting here. I never do."

We started down toward the pond, moving quietly through the big trees, following one of the watercourses. Already we could hear the soft feeding call of mallards. It sounded like a good flock. The old man indicated a fir tree twenty yards ahead, one that was big enough to conceal us both. We approached the tree with the dogs between us. Close against the rough bark we stood and waited. Some of the mallard hens had quacked loudly just as we reached the tree. They had heard us, or perhaps just sensed our presence. No more than twenty feet from the water, we gave them time to settle down. Steller's jays scolded somewhere far above us. It could have been them that warned the mallards.

We knelt. The old man took my gun, then lay both guns behind us. The jays had quieted now. We peered around either side of the tree. Better than a hundred mallards were using the pond, as well as an even dozen Canada geese. The mallards were calm again, some of them tipping to feed, the drakes' green heads and chestnut breasts bright now with fall plumage. Most of the mallards were toward our side, within twenty yards of us. Near the opposite bank, out from the narrow muddy border between the water and the trees, the honkers—apparently six pairs—fed contentedly, with no idea any human was near.

There's an excitement—or something beyond that, a rejuvenation—when you see wild creatures in wild places without your presence being known. We knelt and watched the birds for a long time, and when we finally left, we were careful not to disturb them.

About fifteen minutes later we heard the barrage. It started with about ten quick, sporadic shots, followed by a brief pause broken by the echoes, then another series of shots, these evenly spaced.

The old man swore violently. "The pond!" he said. "Those asshole kids nailed them on the pond!" A third, more widely spaced series of shots began. "The no-good bastards are working on the cripples!"

What followed made me recall the Dylan Thomas lines: "Do not go gentle into that good night. Old age should burn and rave at close of day. Rage, rage against the dying of the light." Ordinarily I mistrust people who claim to think of literature at such moments, but it happened to me then.

We hurried back to the pond, but the young men were long gone. Without a dog, and apparently not wanting to get their feet wet, they had left three mallards and two geese dead on the water. It was impossible to know how many birds they had managed to retrieve.

We hiked back out again, this time with the three grouse plus three ducks and two big geese. The old man swore all the way. We saw no further sign of the young men.

It was a good day gone awful at its ending. When we reached my car, the old man insisted I take the birds, all of them. "Use them," he said. "Never waste birds." He walked away down the Forest Service road in the shade of its surrounding timber, his Lab at heel. He never looked back, and I had no idea how far he had to go.

I did use the birds—their flesh as food and their feathers as trout and steelhead flies. But I never saw the old man again, though I asked around and learned about him. Late that winter I heard he was dead, and I'm certain he did not go gentle into that good night. Whenever I hunted from then on, I thought of him, especially when I passed up easy shots, as he had taught me to do.

Diverse Experiences Large and Small

Birds, not people, are the creatures that most embody life and freedom on earth.
—Yongey Mingyur Rinpoche, *In Love with the World*

I looked down from our deck toward the pond as I was putting out seeds one morning, and saw that an egret had arrived. These long-legged, stately white birds visit throughout the year at unpredictable times of day. This one stood motionless, knee-deep on black legs in shallow water at the far edge of the pond. I knew that by 1900 egrets had been hunted to near extinction for their decorative white plumage—feathers so brilliantly white that, from a distance, they appear to be illuminated. Back then, fashionable women enjoyed wearing such feathers in their hats.

Next, three scrub jays, swooping in from different directions, arrived on the deck railing almost simultaneously and began squawking, flapping their wings, and lunging at one another. After a half-minute skirmish, they resolved their issues. The dominant jay stayed on the railing, one hopped down to the Saint Francis bowl, and the third dropped all the way to the deck to salvage the seeds that had been randomly scattered there.

When a collared dove glided in to land on the railing, the dominant jay allowed it to stay.

Two western bluebirds fluttered out of the tall Douglas-fir and landed on the birdbath facing each other. After a short pause, they both walked into the water and began flapping their wings and splashing with enthusiasm. According to experts, birds bathe both to clean their feathers and to rid themselves of para-

Red-tailed hawk.

sites. I don't dispute experts, but anyone who watches bluebirds can clearly see that they also bathe for fun.

A red-tailed hawk announced itself with a harsh screech, and then, just as I looked up, it landed near the top of the Douglas-fir. Hawks are known to attack feeding songbirds, but we've never seen it happen. In our refuge, for some reason, predators and prey peacefully coexist.

Two years after the old man I'd hunted grouse with died, I returned to the pond where the ducks and geese had been slaughtered. There were no waterfowl this time, but not far from the water I discovered a dead red-tailed hawk lying on its side on a gray, flat-topped rock. Its warm body was limp and clearly hadn't been there long. I examined the bird closely and found no sign of injury anywhere. Dark brown above, lighter brown below, with a white-streaked belly and the cinnamon-colored tail that gave the species its name, there wasn't so much as a ruffled feather. And they were lovely feathers, soft to the touch. I left the hawk on the rock where I found it, just as, for the same reasons, I leave Indian artifacts wherever I happen to find them.

Years ago, bounty hunters in various Oregon counties were paid ten dollars for sets of coyote ears. My handmade wooden predator call imitates the high-pitched screaming of a wounded rabbit, and back then I often used it to call in coyotes, both just to get a close look and in hopes that after being fooled once, they wouldn't fall for a similar call issued by a bounty hunter.

Shortly before dark one summer evening, I was well concealed alongside a creek in a narrow draw thick with oak trees and willow brush. I had used my predator call and a large male coyote was trotting down the creek bank straight at me. My plan, as always, was to let him get within a few yards and then stand, say hello, and watch him stop short, register surprise, and turn to dash away. But this time I was at least as surprised as the coyote, because just as I stood, I heard a piercing screech and felt a sudden rush of air, and a red-tailed hawk knocked my hat off. Hawks eat rabbits too, and this one, undoubtedly surprised and possibly enraged by my subterfuge, screeched again and again as it flew low up the draw to disappear along with the coyote.

All raptors are impressive birds. I find ospreys especially satisfying to watch, probably because, with fish as their principal food, they live in picturesque places near water.

The North Umpqua is an Oregon summer steelhead river with thirty-one miles of its waters designated as fly-angling only. The seagoing rainbow trout begin arriving in June and remain in the river until fall storms, usually in November, draw most of these fish up tributary spawning creeks. Hilde and I have fished and loved the North Umpqua for more than a half century; and for many years we leased an old, secluded house from a friend who owned land—a former homestead—near the heart of the fly water. The house was up a winding dirt road about a quarter mile from the river and had more space than we needed: a living room, two small bedrooms, a kitchen, a bathroom, and a centrally located woodstove. Just a few yards beyond the front door was a quarter-acre pond with largemouth bass and bluegills in it. We never fished the pond, but an osprey did.

Early morning and evenings—when there's shade on the water—are the best times to fly-fish for steelhead, and that left us free to do whatever we wanted through the long summer days. We had electricity but no telephone or television set, and the radio picked up distant stations only after dark. So besides books and each other, birds were our main source of entertainment; and the osprey that visited, undoubtedly flying up the hill from the river, was our favorite.

But there were other birds, too. One year we watched a pair of robins build their nest on the sill outside our bedroom window. The handsome, red-breasted male did his share of the work but took occasional breaks to fight his reflection in the window glass. Both birds sometimes sang through the night, accompanied by crickets and frogs. One morning in mid-June when we came back from fishing, there were six pale blue eggs in the cuplike nest. For about two weeks the female incubated the eggs, and for another two weeks after they hatched, both parents fed the perpetually hungry fledglings. Five of the young survived, with one left dead in the abandoned nest.

Every year, one or two pairs of wood ducks nested in cavities in nearby trees. Within a day after hatching, the babies would jump from their nest, landing either on the ground or in the pond. For the next two months, we'd watch the ducklings as they closely followed their mothers, learning to feed on aquatic plants and insects.

Though bats are mammals whose forelimbs serve as wings, they fly as well as any small bird, and better than most. During our summers on the North Umpqua, we watched them hunt insects over the pond just before dark, acrobatically swooping, swerving, and darting after their prey. For some reason they also liked to fly from room to room inside our porous house late at night, when we were in bed. The first time it happened I woke up feeling a rush of air and aware of a fluttering sound. When I sat up, I saw the bat speeding back and forth between me and the moonlit window, missing my head by an inch or two each time it passed. As Hilde slept soundly, I turned on a bedside lamp and got up. By then the bat had left the room, and I followed after it, turning on lights all over the house as I went.

I walked from room to room until I found it attached to a bathroom wall, not far below the ceiling. Retrieving a pot from the kitchen, I used the lid to gently scrape the bat into the pot and covered it. When I carried the pot out the front door and raised the lid, the little winged mammal flew away at once, making the same fluttering sound it had awakened me with.

"Don't hurry back," I said.

If that one didn't come back, others did, one at a time; and I was always happy to remove them from whatever wall I found them on and release them outside in the dead of night. Dracula and other myths have given bats a bad name, and it's true that large numbers of them live in close quarters and carry viruses. But they're also useful creatures. Just like bees, they pollinate plants. They consume enough insects to save billions of dollars per year in pest-control costs. For example, in one hour a single bat can devour up to a thousand mosquitoes. Though not as widely celebrated as it should be, Bat Appreciation Day falls on April seventeenth.

Year after year in mid-September—five months after Bat Appreciation Day, that is—the osprey appeared over our North Umpqua pond at midday. Ospreys infrequently eat birds and small mammals as well as fish, but the wood ducks were long gone by then, and after lunch Hilde and I sat on the front steps of the house hoping to see the bird dive. It didn't happen often, but the spectacular show was always worth the wait.

This osprey had a wingspan of at least five feet, with a clearly defined brown necklace across the white chest that marked her as a female. She seemed capable of circling endlessly and effort-

Osprey.

lessly, forty or fifty feet over the pond. After spotting a fish she loosed a shrill screech, hovered briefly, then plunged feet-first into the pond with a huge, loud splash. Powerful wingbeats lifted her out of the water quickly and, clutching a bluegill or bass in her talons, she flew across the pond to disappear into the trees.

When we'd begun fishing the North Umpqua in the 1960s, an osprey was a rare sight. The reasons for that were simple, if difficult to spell: DDT (dichlorodiphenyltrichloroethane) and PCBs (polychlorinated biphenyls) that were in the systems of the raptors' prey made the shells of their eggs so thin that they were crushed when the adult birds nested on them. After the EPA finally banned DDT in 1972 and PCBs in 1979, raptor populations everywhere began a strong recovery.

Back in Ashland, Hilde and I were sitting out on our deck with coffee on a calm, cloudy Sunday morning. The seeds were out, pancake pieces intermixed, but half an hour passed with no birds in sight anywhere, and no birdsong to be heard even from a distance. We wondered if an earthquake might be imminent, possibly even the so-called "big one" predicted to devastate the Northwest sooner or later. Once while visiting my mother in southern California on our way to Baja, we'd awakened to realize that the birds that always made an early racket out back weren't making a sound. Then the earthquake hit. A few years later in Costa Rica we'd also awakened to eerie silence, and seconds later our bed began to shake. Sometimes the birds know more than we do.

So it came as a relief when, finally, a red-shafted flicker glided onto the birdbath to drink. Soon after the flicker left, three western bluebirds took its place. They almost always come in groups and always bathe, usually together. While the bluebirds soaked themselves and splashed, a dozen or so noisy red-wing blackbirds dropped from an oak to the deck railing for seeds. An egret circled the pond down the hill three times on its long, broad wings, then glided down to station itself in shallow water. When I looked back at the deck railing, the blackbirds were gone and three juncos were feeding on the seeds. A scrub jay came by and stopped long enough to fill his beak with pancake pieces.

On a dead-calm Baja morning twenty years ago, Hilde and I beached our small aluminum boat—twelve feet long, powered by a 15-horsepower engine—on the backside of Carmen Island. We were twelve miles offshore east of Loreto and had come to explore a long, broad, lonely beach.

Hilde went one way and I went the other. I found some shells and then, just above the high tide line, discovered the fragile, five-foot long shed skin of a diamond-backed rattlesnake. While I was admiring the snakeskin and wondering how nearby its former occupant might be, I heard a tern chirping. Looking up, I saw it down the beach, circling over shallow water on its long white wings.

Soon I was close enough to make out the bird's black head and orange bill. When I was almost underneath the circling tern, it stopped short to hover in place. After a few seconds it plunged into the water, came up with a wriggling sardine, and flew directly at me on the beach. Unless you're feeding them, seabirds are shy, so I expected the tern to flare away with its prey to eat in peace and privacy elsewhere on the beach. Instead, it dropped the sardine back into the sea and landed on the white sand a few feet from where I stood, looking up at me with small black eyes.

I looked back. "Sorry," I said. "You lost"—I looked at my watch—"your late breakfast or your early lunch."

The tern stepped toward me, cutting the distance between us in half by the time it stopped.

"Are you mad?" I asked. "Disappointed? Dumb?"

Black-crested head tilted to one side, it looked straight up at me.

When a long line of brown pelicans flew by close to shore a few yards over the water, we both looked briefly in that direction, then back at each other.

The tern stepped closer.

"I don't think you're dumb," I said. "Maybe you never saw a human being before. Is that it?"

Up the beach, close to our boat, four pelicans left their line to climb, then circle and dive, crashing into the calm water. They'd spotted a school of sardines, and the others circled to dive down after them.

When I looked back at the tern, it was close enough for me to lean down and try to touch it.

The little bird showed no fear. I dropped my shells, picked it up gently, and cradled it, damp and warm, in my hands. The black-tipped wings raised, then lowered to cover my hands. I remembered Alejandro and the myna bird in Manoa Valley, nearly fifty years back.

"That must be it," I said. "You've never seen a person before."

It stared at me, and its orange beak opened and closed.

"You sure don't weigh much. Are you all right? Do you know how lucky you are to be able to fly?"

When I raised my cupped hands above my head, it flew off at once, heading north, the same way the pelicans had gone.

I'd saved a sardine and, in my mind, made a temporary friend.

On another day in Baja, Hilde and I stopped our boat on the far side of Carmen to cast streamer flies at a floating line of Sargasso seaweed, hoping for dorado.

The fish were there under the seaweed, and Hilde soon hooked and landed a fifteen-pound bull. As most landed dorado do, this one made many acrobatic jumps, golden sides flashing bright in sunlight. I finally gripped the wrist of its tail, lifted the fish out of the water, and laid it across my knees. As I did so, a live and apparently healthy sardine popped out of its mouth, bounced off the gunwale and into the water, righted itself, then swam away. A few seconds later, with the barbless hook removed, I returned the dorado to the sea as well.

"We all deserve second chances," Hilde said.

"All of us?"

"Most of us."

"Yes. For sure."

Two hours later, having landed and released three more dorados from underneath the seaweed line, we headed back to camp. On our run to shore we saw schools of bottlenose dolphins, a blue whale, flying fish, gulls and pelicans diving for schools of sardines, and high-flying frigate birds.

Once ashore with the boat moored, we drove the dusty road to Loreto to shop for fruit, vegetables, and Dos Equis beer at the town's only grocery store. Then we visited a bakery that could only be reached by walking through a chicken coop. We bought bread and breakfast rolls, and the young woman who sold the baked goods totaled up our bill by writing with an index finger on a breadboard dusted with flour.

It was our lucky day, because after obtaining the bread from the bakery, the icehouse also had ice and the gas station had gas.

Baja tern.

Back at camp, we cached our supplies in the tent and sat out-side in the shade to enjoy our cold beers. No, it wasn't luxurious living—or even comfortable living by most people's standards—which was one reason we loved it.

White-winged doves and a covey of quail visited our camp-site regularly, even while we were sitting outside the tent in plain sight. Roadrunners made infrequent appearances. Late one night I woke up and saw, just a few feet away, a kit fox sniffing at the breadbox. Tarantulas and scorpions also occasionally showed up at camp; and on one evening run along the lonely Baja highway, I spotted a coiled diamondback at the edge of the road barely in time to jump over it and spin around to warn Hilde.

The relatively primitive conditions we enjoyed during our Baja visits often brought to mind Aldo Leopold's observation in *A Sand County Almanac* that "[r]ecreation is valuable in pro-portion to the intensity of the experiences, and to the degree to which it differs from and contrasts with workaday life."

And in turn, Leopold's aphorism calls to mind a vulgar modern antithesis to our own experience, a so-called recreational vehicle I read about somewhere: the Marchi Mobile eleMMent palazzo Superior motorhome, featuring a retractable rooftop deck, leather-clad rotating loungers, wireless control of everything from the temperature to the security cameras, a living room that lifts to become a full bar, a fireplace, two flat-screen TVs, and a push-button retractable skydeck with a heated floor. With a 510-horsepower diesel engine, the vehicle can hit ninety-three miles per hour on the open road—and all this for a mere three million dollars.

Hilde and I were happy with our battered Ford Bronco and a tent.

We didn't encounter any Marchi Mobile eleMMents when we drove home the week after I met the tern. Northwest of San Ignacio, however, about halfway to Guerrero Negro and with nothing but the Sonoran Desert to be seen in any direction, we did come upon four young men—one of them holding a shovel and another a pick—standing alongside the road, which was as lonely as the Carmen Island beach.

As we approached in the Bronco, they tried to wave us down. They were a tough-looking bunch, and I was with a lovely woman out in the true middle of nowhere. I knew I should drive by, and at first I did. But then, feeling guilt, I stopped, backed up, and rolled my window down.

"Que pasa?"

"No hay agua," one of them said. "Necesitamos agua."

Hilde's Spanish was far better than mine, and she talked to them and got their story. A man who was supposed to pick them up was more than two hours late. They had buried a close friend in a grave in the desert. The day was very hot, even hotter than usual, and they badly needed water. We had three plastic gallon-jugs and gave them two. They took turns with the first jug and drained it quickly. As they drank, a flight of white-winged doves crossed the road and then veered sharply to land behind the men between two tall saguaro cacti.

"Es suficiente agua?" Hilde asked.

"Si. Nuestro aventon vendrá. Tenemos las palomas para compañia."

"Buena suerte," Hilde said.

All four waved and smiled as we drove away.

"What did he say?" I asked Hilde.

"That they'd be fine. They have the doves for company."

Four cedar waxwings, a species we'd seldom seen in recent years, arrived late in the morning and perched around the edge of the birdbath to drink. I was glad I'd scrubbed the bath and filled it with fresh water the previous evening. Within seconds the waxwings were joined by two scrub jays, four acorn woodpeckers, and five western bluebirds. The bluebirds walked into the water; the woodpeckers chased the bluebirds out; and then the jays chased both the woodpeckers and cedar waxwings away. But none of the birds would leave the area. The battle —and it was one—lasted thirty or forty seconds. According to their natures, the jays and

Cedar waxwing.

woodpeckers were loud and aggressive while the waxwings and bluebirds, smaller and quicker in flight, executed evasive actions. And then the conflict ended. Suddenly, all fifteen birds—I counted twice—were peacefully integrated and evenly spaced, circling the water. They drank together, and then took turns bathing two or three at a time.

A 2019 article in *Science* magazine reported a 29 percent decline in North American bird life—nearly three billion birds—between 1970 and 2017, largely due to climate change, insecticides, and habitat destruction. It's also been reported that the meadowlark, Oregon's state bird, has declined by 139 million, and the dark-eyed junco by 168 million. Hilde and I live in what are classified as oak grasslands—prime bird habitat—and we're well aware of the drastic reduction in the number of waxwings and juncos visiting our property, as well as the virtual disappearance of the western meadowlark.

Responding to the *Science* article in a local paper, John Alexander, cofounder and executive director of Ashland's Klamath Bird Observatory, noted that "[b]irds are one of the best indicators of environmental health. They are the canary (in the coal mine). This signals that natural systems are being severely degraded by human activity."

The same week that the bad news about birds came out in *Science*, Swedish sixteen-year-old Greta Thunberg, in her speech to world leaders at the United Nations, put things more forcefully: "My message is that we'll be watching you. . . . You have stolen my dreams and my childhood with your empty words. And yet I'm one of the lucky ones. People are suffering. People are dying. Entire ecosystems are collapsing . . . and all you can talk about is money, and fairy tales of eternal economic growth. How dare you!"

Indeed.

Dark-eyed junco.

We spent a spring vacation with our daughter and two grandsons in Zihuatanejo on Mexico's Pacific coast. Grandson Billy, fourteen at the time, went parasailing one afternoon while the rest of us watched from the beach. Towed by a power boat far beneath him, Billy sailed a mile north along the coast, then made a sweeping turn and came back over the blue sea to land safely on the white sand beach, no more than fifty yards from a pond of crocodiles.

With Billy's urging, I decided to make the same trip the next afternoon.

Two young Mexican men buckled heavy leather harnesses around my chest and shoulders and gave me directions on how to control my descent at the end of the flight. Then I was lifted smoothly off the warm sand and sailed out over the ocean. The great surprise was that, within seconds, I was so high over the sea that nothing below me could be heard, not even the sound of the powerful motor pulling me along.

All I felt was warm wind in my face, and all I saw was the blue sky and the darker blue sea beneath me—until the frigate birds appeared. Every day from the beach, or from chest-deep water as we waited with our boogie boards for a set of good waves, I'd watched the frigate birds circling high out over deep water. These that now appeared seemed to materialize from nowhere, six of them, three on each side, only yards away. For the first time in my life, I saw them up close and clearly—their iridescent black feathers, long downward-curving beaks, red throat patches, and white bellies.

I sailed a mile north and then, after a long, slow turn, back toward my starting point. The frigate birds stayed with me. For the first and probably last time in a long life I was up with the birds, far above cars, concrete, corruption, contagion, disease. The exhilaration I felt in that moment will live as long as I do. And if I were ever forced to decide whether to spend the rest of my life in a Marchi Mobile eleMMent palazzo Superior or be transformed into a frigate bird, the choice would be easy.

Epilogue

I was mowing the front lawn in early July during the pandemic, when a familiar brown and white cat from across the road appeared no more than fifteen feet away, creeping straight at me through high green grass. Staring straight ahead, it crouched and waggled its hindquarters, ready to pounce. Then I noticed the pair of grounded fledgling scrub jays between the predator and me, and I killed the lawnmower motor, screamed at the cat, and gently grabbed a bird in each hand. Ordinarily, fledglings that fall from nests or trees are best left alone because they're likely under the close observation of their parents. But I studied the area closely and neither saw nor heard adult jays anywhere, and no nest was in sight in either of two nearby Douglas-firs. I was certain the cat would soon be back—it hunted the territory regularly—and knew that raccoons would also be out during the night.

So I carried the birds into the house and showed them to Hilde.

We named the jays Heckle and Jeckle, after two cartoon characters—talking magpies—that, along with the Roadrunner, were popular when I was young. We lined a large laundry basket with newsprint, then spread grass over the newsprint and wedged in short oak tree branches to serve as perches. An old window screen became the roof.

Every other day, we hosed down the laundry basket and changed the newspaper and grass. In the beginning, every two to three hours from dawn to dusk, we fed Heckle and Jeckle canned cat food using a wooden martini pick, and gave them water with an eyedropper. During the daylight hours they stayed on the deck in the shade. From dusk to dawn, they slept in a spare room perched side by side. I hoped that their bond to each other would remain stronger than their connection to us.

We steadily increased the interval between feedings and eventually left their provisions in an empty cat food can in their basket, giving them no choice but to learn to eat on their own. Every morning and evening we let them flutter and then fly around their bedroom as best they could, perching between flights on a bookcase, the arms of chairs, and the back of a couch.

They made quick, steady progress. Heckle was the larger and stronger of the pair from the start and appeared to be ready for life in the wild after about three weeks. We thought that getting a wild creature back to where it belonged as quickly as possible would lead to the best possible outcome. On a warm Monday morning, I carried him in cupped hands as Hilde and I crossed the back yard to stand between two oak trees favored by our scrub jay colony.

"Good luck," I said. "You're ready. You can do this."

When I opened my hands, Heckle flew up robustly, perched on a high limb, turned with a hop to look down at us, then squawked much like a mature jay. As we turned away and walked back toward the house, the squawking continued. Early the next morning, as I scattered seeds on the deck railing, Heckle, not quite fully grown and easily recognizable, suddenly landed an arm's length away, the first bird to arrive. Silent now, he began pecking up seeds.

"Way to go," I said. "Good for you."

A few days later we released Jeckle, also in mid-morning. For that day and the next, whenever I went outside for any reason, Jeckle emerged from the oaks and landed somewhere near me, sometimes on my right shoulder. When those reunions stopped on the third day, I found myself somewhat sad, but largely happy and relieved.

Scrub jay with cat food can.

Both birds have adapted to their proper lives, and along with the other resident jays they peck at acorns, patrol the yard for insects, eat the seeds we provide, drink from the birdbath, and, whenever they feel the need or the urge, they fly free.

August 9, 2020